100 Years Up High

COLORADO MOUNTAINS & MOUNTAINEERS

100 Years Up High

COLORADO MOUNTAINS & MOUNTAINEERS

Janet Neuhoff Robertson | James E. Fell, Jr. | David Hite | Christopher J. Case | Walter R. Borneman

THE COLORADO MOUNTAIN CLUB PRESS
GOLDEN COLORADO

100 Years Up High: *Colorado Mountains & Mountaineers*

Partial funding for this book was made possible by the
Neuhoff Book Fund of the Colorado Mountain Club Foundation.

PUBLISHED BY:

The Colorado Mountain Club Press
710 10th Street, Suite 200, Golden, CO 80401
303-279-3080 | 800-633-4417
EMAIL: cmcpress@cmc.org | WEBSITE: http://www.cmc.org

Alan Bernhard: designer, compositor, and production manager
Joyce Dunne: copyeditor
David Hite: photo editor
Alan Stark: publisher

FRONT COVER PHOTO: Capitol Peak panorama, Elk Mountains, by Greg Parent
BACK COVER PHOTO: Lupine and the Sneffels Range, by Glenn Randall

DISTRIBUTED TO THE BOOK TRADE BY:

Mountaineers Books
1001 SW Klickitat Way, Suite 201, Seattle, WA 98134
800-553-4453 | www.mountaineersbooks.org

We gratefully acknowledge the financial support of the people of Colorado through the Scientific and Cultural Facilities District of greater metropolitan Denver for our publishing activities.

First Edition

ISBN 978-0-9842213-9-4

Printed in Korea

To those who have come before,

and those we know will follow.

Sunrise on Longs Peak.
Courtesy of Colorado Mountain Club Archives.

Maroon Peak from West Maroon Basin.
Indian paintbrush and other flowers light up a high-country
slope in the Maroon Bells Wilderness Area near Aspen.

Photograph by Glenn Randall. Courtesy of Glenn Randall.

CONTENTS

Sunrise on Eolus, North Eolus, Turret, Pigeon, and Monitor Peaks, as seen from Sunlight Peak.

Photograph by Glenn Randall. Courtesy of Glenn Randall.

CELEBRATION AND TRIBUTE

THIS BOOK IS A CELEBRATION OF THE 100TH ANNIVERSARY of the Colorado Mountain Club and a tribute to its role in mountaineering in Colorado and beyond. From the beginning of the project, our overarching goal was to focus on the powerful changes that encompassed all phases of Colorado mountaineering in the first century of the club's history and to share with you the benchmarks and achievements that have made mountaineering a lifetime passion for so many.

The club's mission today is what it was when it was founded in 1912. It continues to be the engine that powers our ability to collect and distribute information regarding the Rocky Mountains on behalf of science, literature, art, and recreation, and to encourage the preservation of forests, flowers, fauna, and natural scenery.

We want to thank everyone who assisted in the project. Woody Smith, Colorado Mountain Club historian and long-time member, contributed significant time and knowledge in helping David Hite research, gather, photograph, and catalog images in the club archives. David's efforts were facilitated by the unhesitating cooperative spirit of artists, photographers, museums, libraries, and private collectors in Colorado and throughout the country. Alan Stark, publisher of the Colorado Mountain Club Press, provided valuable editorial direction. And the Colorado Mountain Club Foundation provided generous support for publication. We trust that this work will be a fitting commemoration of both the Colorado Mountain Club's first century and the development of mountaineering over the course of that time.

Janet N. Robertson | James E. Fell, Jr. | David Hite | Christopher J. Case | Walter R. Borneman

Grenadier Range. Climbing in the San Juan Mountains presents one of
the greatest challenges and adventures for Colorado mountaineers.

Photograph by David Anschicks. Courtesy of David Anschicks.

SETTING THE STAGE

JAMES E. FELL, JR.

*At the top we halted in frozen admiration. Mountain range
after mountain range succeeded one another, rising and falling
like storm-driven waves, cresting with streamers of snow
blowing straight out from each icy perpendicular 14,000-foot
peak. In all that landscape of rock, snow, and ice, there was
neither print of animal nor track of man. We were alone as
though the world had just been created and we were its first
inhabitants.*

—Elizabeth Paepcke

———

Elizabeth Paepcke and her friends were neither the first nor the last to see
the grand and remote landscape they had trekked to, but her memory of this
particular ascent to the summit of Aspen Mountain in 1938 captured the
essence of the Rocky Mountains and the emotions of innumerable mountaineers before and since.

People have lived in the region for at least 12,000 years since the end of the
Ice Age. From the first, the mountains—their space, their slopes, their close
and distant presence—have focused that experience, as a place to live, a place
to enjoy, a place to wonder, a place to inspire.

The role the mountains played in the lives of the first ancient peoples
coming from Asia is known only in outline. They discovered the passes and

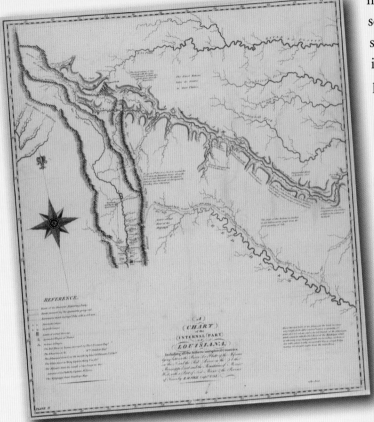

Pike's Map. In 1806, Lieutenant Zebulon Montgomery Pike and 20 men traveled across the plains in a daring attempt to find the headwaters of the Red River and thereby determine the western boundary of the United States. This map, entitled "Chart of the Internal Part of Louisiana," which shows Highest Peak (later to become Pikes Peak), accompanied the expedition's official report published in 1810.

Courtesy of the collection of Wes Brown.

made the first summits. They hiked to and through the mountains in search of food—they were hunters and gatherers—and they used the summits to scout, the passes to travel, and special trails to trap prey in high country. As they developed pictographs, petroglyphs, and pottery, some of which survive to this day, they depicted the mountains—meaning that art was part of their culture. They left artifacts behind on many a summit, and they appear to have used the mountains for ceremonial purposes. At least one legend—that of the Old Man Gun, a 19th-century Arapaho—relates the story of a man who climbed to the summit of Longs Peak to snare eagles for feathers used in part for spiritual purposes. But overall, without written language, the story of these earliest peoples in the mountains has largely disappeared.

Modern mountaineering in what became Colorado developed with Spanish soldiers, explorers, and adventurers. Moving north from present-day New Mexico in the 1600s and 1700s, they explored the high plains and ventured into the mountains. They learned of passes from the Indian peoples—mostly the Utes—and they searched for gold and silver and for non-desert routes to California. They named, or more accurately, renamed, the rivers, mountains, and ranges—names that survive to this day—and they trekked across the plains using key peaks—notably Pikes Peak—as landmarks to guide their journeys. In the later 1700s and after, the Spanish combined art and exploration in creating the first maps of the region—mostly of southern and western Colorado, which formed the northern limits of the Spanish Empire, a vast and diverse land stretching all the way to the tip of South America.

Mountaineering in the Rockies grew dramatically in the 19th century. In 1803, the young United States made the famous Louisiana

Purchase, doubling the size of the national domain and acquiring part of the future Colorado—the lands north and east of the Arkansas River. Explorers, fur trappers, and traders quickly moved in, and with that, the American mountaineering experience in the Rockies began. In 1806–1807, Lieutenant Zebulon M. Pike made a still-controversial reconnaissance of the region. Sometime after his troops "gave three cheers to the Mexican mountains"—they were also known then as the Snowy Mountains and the Stony Mountains—he tried and failed to climb what he called the Grand Peak, the mountain that bears his name today. Winter ascents were difficult then, as now, and two days without food and the waist-deep snow ended his efforts.

Continuing westward, he eventually camped in the San Luis Valley until Spanish troops arrived and "invited" his frozen, starving party to Santa Fe. Ultimately, the Spanish confiscated Pike's journal and extensive map work of the region, but he stored synopses of his work in the musket barrels of his troops, studied Mexican maps provided in Chihuahua by Juan Pedro Walker, and from these in 1810 emerged his book *An Account of Expeditions to the Sources of the Mississippi and through the Western Parts of Louisiana*. There, he famously described the plains region as a land that "may become in time equally celebrated as the sandy deserts of Africa." Translated into French, Dutch, and German, Pike's work made him the most important early explorer of Louisiana, although the Lewis and Clark Expedition has received the lion's share of the fame. The latter was far less important, however, because Meriwether Lewis never published the exploration's report. The United States and the world first learned of the Rocky Mountain region through the work of Zebulon Pike.[1]

Other explorers expanded on Pike's efforts. In 1820, Major Stephen Harriman Long of the US Army led what was known as the Yellow Stone Expedition across the plains from Council Bluffs in Iowa and initially mistook

Ready for the Slopes.
With no heat, no radio, no ski racks, this Model T Ford, owned by a member of the Colorado Mountain Club, prepared to head to the slopes with skis and toboggan around 1916.

Courtesy of Colorado Mountain Club Archives.

Ten Mile Valley. An English-born painter recovering from tuberculosis, Harry Learned captured an early train steaming through the Ten Mile Valley and the old mining town of Robinson, Colorado, on its way to Leadville. This scene is entirely gone today. Tailings from Bartlett Peak at the upper right, the world's largest known molybdenum deposit, fill the entire valley in front of the painter, an area now in reclamation.

Untitled. Painting by Harry Learned. Private Collection.
Photograph courtesy of Neal R. Smith Fine Art.

the great mountain in today's Rocky Mountain National Park for Pike's Grand Peak. Moving south along the Front Range of the Rockies, Long's artists, Titian Peale and Samuel Seymour, painted the first images of the region and its key features. Long's botanist, Edwin James, and others made the first known ascent of what would soon be called Pikes Peak, though at the summit they found Indian artifacts and realized that they were hardly the first to have reached it. Long, James, and others subsequently published the so-called *Long Report* in the early 1820s. It provided better maps and delineated the region in greater detail than Pike's publication had and, building on Pike's, created the myth of the plains region east of the mountains as "the Great American Desert." This name remained on maps worldwide until the end of the 19th century and still reflects ways in which people characterize the area.[2]

If early government explorers confined themselves mostly to the high plains and Front Range, fur trappers penetrated the mountains in search of beaver skins. They "discovered" the passes, traced the rivers to their sources, and searched out the landscape. They named the Blue, Green, and White rivers. As the fur trade died away, trappers led a second generation of government explorers, such as John C. Fremont and John W. Gunnison, across the mountains in explorations designed to provide more accurate maps than were previously available and find railroad routes for the iron horse. Artists such as Richard Kern created additional images, and early travelers including Sir St. George Gore initiated the first known climbing for aesthetics and sport and lent their names to the landscape as well. And in the Treaty of Guadalupe Hidalgo, which ended the Mexican War in 1848, the United States acquired the modern Southwest and with it the lands south and west of the Arkansas River, which comprise that part of modern-day Colorado.

But it was the Pikes Peak Gold Rush that created both Colorado and modern mountaineering. As early as 1858, the boom launched by gold discoveries at Denver City, Kansas Territory, and elsewhere prompted thousands of argonauts to rush across the plains to the junction of Cherry Creek and the South Platte River. Though gold drew them west, many boomers marveled at the mountain backdrop, and discoveries beyond the Front Range drew them into the high country. And they began climbing.

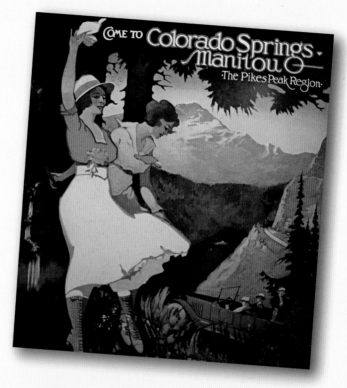

By Train and by Car. By the 1930s, mountaineering in all its forms had become part of Colorado's tourist economy. These exuberant women frolic in the woods, perhaps to entice the men in the car driving up the road to the summit of Pikes Peak in this poster from the 1930s.

Courtesy of Colorado Springs Pioneers Museum.

Hayden Survey. Guide Harry Yount stands at the top of Berthoud Pass during the 1874 Hayden Survey.

Photograph by William Henry Jackson.
Courtesy of Neal R. Smith Fine Art.

In August 1858, Julia Holmes, heading to the placer mines wearing moccasins and her risqué bloomer outfit, became the first woman known to have climbed Pikes Peak. "I have accomplished the task which I marked out for myself," she wrote at the summit. And she marveled at the landscape: "Extending as far as the eye can reach lie the great level plains, stretched out in all their verdure and beauty while the winding of the grand Arkansas is visible for many miles." She mused. "Here I am, and feel that I would not have missed this glorious sight for anything at all."[3]

Innumerable others expressed the same sentiments, but not everyone. Isabella Bird, the professional English traveler, remembered "six hours of terror" that were "never to be forgotten" when she climbed Longs Peak via the Keyhole Route in 1873. Aesthetics, fear, and relief went hand in hand for some climbers.[4]

The gold rush also delineated the so-called Colorado mineral belt, a great oval that ran across the mountains from the Indian Peaks in the northeast to the San Juan Mountains in the southwest. This concept was important, as the developing mining industry in the high country would also define mountaineering in Colorado from the time of the gold rush until the early 20th century. Exploration and development carried miners above timberline. Some turned into hikers and climbers, and the roads, bridges, and railroads built to serve the industry provided mountaineers with easier access than was otherwise possible.

Photographers made their way west in the gold rush and captured the first images of the mountains, sometimes out of the photographer's personal interest and sometimes for the great federal surveys that succeeded the army explorations of pre-territorial days. The most famous of these efforts were the Wheeler and Hayden surveys in the San Juan Mountains of the early 1870s, both of which outlined potential mining ground, mapped and surveyed the land, and brought in photographers such as William Henry Jackson. Members of these survey teams made some of the first known ascents in the rugged San Juan Mountains in the course of their professional work.

Artists came as well. Like the photographers, some painted the mountains for personal interest and occasional profit, but others reflected the key artistic tradition of the age, the Hudson River School, which found the ideal of American wilderness in the mountains of the West. Among these painters, Thomas Worthington Whittredge

Summiteers on Longs Peak. Coats and ties for men and full skirts for women were the proper attire for hikers and climbers in class-conscious late Victorian and early 20th-century America.

Photograph courtesy of Denver Public Library.

3201. MT OF THE HOLY CROSS. W.H.J. & C?

Mount of the Holy Cross. This is considered to be the most famous photograph of 19th-century Colorado. It embodied the belief of so many in God's grace on the new republic.

Photograph by William Henry Jackson.
Courtesy of Denver Public Library.

captured the high plains set against a dramatic mountain background. The artist Albert Bierstadt made the first known ascent of Mount Evans. Later, the federal government renamed Mount Bierstadt after the painter.

While the new wagon roads and the rough stagecoaches that used them boosted hiking and climbing, it was railroad construction to support mining that opened the slopes for mountaineers still more. The Colorado Central, along with the Denver South Park & Pacific, the Denver and Rio Grande, and other lines, hammered down rails

Mount Eolus. Though better known for his paintings of
the Front Range, Charles Partridge Adams here depicted
Mount Eolus in the San Juan Mountains.

Painting by Charles Partridge Adams.
Courtesy of Dusty and Kathy Loo Historic Colorado Collection.

throughout the Front Range, South Park, and the Central Rockies. The short line roads developed by Otto Mears, the so-called pathfinder of the San Juans, also opened up southwestern Colorado for mining and mountaineering.

In tandem with railroad construction was the development of the first great tourist resorts and hotels along the Front Range by the builders of the Rio Grande, notably General William Jackson Palmer, founder of Colorado Springs, a city designed to be the "Newport in the Rockies," a name reflecting the fashionable summer resort for the New York elite at Newport, Rhode Island.

By the end of the 19th century, the Gilded Age gave rise to powerful new reform movements across the nation—preservation and conservation—both of which would have a huge impact on mountaineering in the Centennial State. The idea of preservation reflected the philosophy of John Muir of California and others who articulated the idea that mountains and other scenic and natural wonders were worth preserving for their own sake. The concept of conservation evolved around the ideas of Gifford Pinchot of Pennsylvania and others who advocated conserving America's natural resources so they could be used by future generations and put to their best use for the people as a whole.

Muir's idea of preservation nurtured the growing national park movement. Congress created Yellowstone National Park in Wyoming and Montana in 1872, followed by Yosemite National Park in California and Mesa Verde National Park in Colorado. Eventually, Congress created the National Park Service in 1916 to manage the system.

The idea of conservation evolved in the 1890s, when the administrations of Benjamin Harrison and William McKinley began withdrawing certain public lands from entry, a policy greatly expanded by McKinley's successor, Theodore Roosevelt, an outdoor and fitness enthusiast who enjoyed travel through Colorado. Gifford Pinchot was his close friend and supporter. Responding more to Pinchot and less to Muir, Roosevelt persuaded Congress to create the US Forest Service, with its conservation and best use philosophy, in 1906. Pinchot became its first director and the first national forester.

At the dawn of the 20th century, financially and politically, Colorado was the most important state between the Missouri River and California and north of Texas. As had been true since earliest times, central to life in Colorado were its mountains, soon to become an inherent part of the new lifestyles of the 20th century.

Solo. A self-portrait inspired by the
artist's descent of Mount Achonee.

Painting by James Disney. Courtesy of James Disney.

Garden of the Gods. One of the most famous features of the Front Range, the Garden of the Gods at Colorado Springs has attracted artists from earliest times. A remnant of ancient seas in the region, these sandstone uplifts form a key element along the foothills of the Rockies. The artist interprets them here from an unusual angle with Cheyenne Mountain in the background.

Painting by M. L. Weston. Courtesy of Kirkland Museum of Fine & Decorative Art, Denver.

Climbing Pikes Peak. Climbers from the AdAmAn Club of Colorado Springs brace against the swirling winds and snow while ascending the cog railroad. Each year members climb Pikes Peak to set off fireworks on New Year's Eve.

Photograph by Harry Standley. Courtesy of Colorado Springs Pioneers Museum.

Longs Peak. Though best known for his interpretations of the Grand Canyon, Merrill Mahaffey turned his hand to other regions as well. This dramatic painting of Longs Peak and the famous Diamond, standing high over Chasm Lake, hangs in the state capitol in Denver.

Painting by Merrill Mahaffey. Courtesy of the House of Representatives, State of Colorado.

CHAPTER 1

CREATING A NEW CLUB AND A NEW NATIONAL PARK

JANET N. ROBERTSON

[T]he most strenuous and unpleasant struggle that I was ever connected with.

—JAMES GRAFTON ROGERS, describing the fight
to create Rocky Mountain National Park

———⊶⋙⟨⟩⋘⊷———

It's no coincidence that the Colorado Mountain Club and Rocky Mountain National Park were created within a few years of each other. Each was championed by the same dedicated group of service-minded, outdoor-oriented people.

One encounters various passionate opinions as to who had the idea to start the Colorado Mountain Club, founded in 1912. Patricia Fazio, who conducted extensive research for her master's thesis, credits Enos Mills with the concept. She cites a letter he wrote on July 24, 1911, to a Denver lawyer named James Grafton Rogers. In the letter, Mills thanks Rogers for agreeing to take the lead in forming a mountain climbing club, suggesting only that he request bylaws from the Appalachian and Sierra clubs. Three days later, Rogers replied by letter, saying he would "take up at least part of the burden" but that the real process of the organization would be delayed "until the mountain climbers have returned from their vacations."

James Grafton Rogers. A Denver attorney and man of many talents, Rogers led the Colorado Mountain Club in its first years and was a major force in the creation of Rocky Mountain National Park.

Courtesy of Colorado Mountain Club Archives.

However, in later reminiscences, neither Rogers nor Mary S. Sabin mentioned Enos Mills. Instead, they politely gave each other credit for starting the Colorado Mountain Club. What is known is that Rogers and Sabin sent out invitations to a meeting that was held on April 3, 1912, at the home of Mrs. Junius F. Brown at 933 Pennsylvania Street in Denver, where Sabin was staying. Seven people accepted the invitation, gathering to discuss the possibility of forming a club that would "make the best of Colorado's most striking resource—its mountains." On April 26, meeting at the same location, 25 people convened to organize what would become the Colorado Mountain Club (CMC), electing officers and forming committees. On May 30, the CMC conducted its first official trip, a hike to the top of South Boulder Peak.

At the time of the club's creation, Rogers was just beginning his remarkable career. He would teach law at Yale University, serve as assistant secretary of state in the Hoover administration, and become dean of the law school at the University of Denver and at the University of Colorado. He would serve as president of the Colorado Mountain Club and, later, of the American Alpine Club.[1]

Mary Sabin was no slouch, either. Born in 1869, she and her younger sister, Florence, started life in Central City. Growing up motherless and poor, they still managed to receive excellent educations. After Sabin graduated from Smith College in 1891, she turned down an assistantship in astronomy at her alma mater, opting to teach math at East High School in Denver so she could help finance her sister's education.

In 1911, Sabin wrote a series of articles about the possibility of forming a mountain club, which were published in the *Rocky Mountain News*. In one letter she described a hike with Florence: "My sister and I went to the [Longs Peak] Inn for the purpose of climbing Long's Peak.

The Loch. After decades of effort, in 2009, the Colorado Mountain Club was instrumental in convincing the federal government to designate the backcountry of Rocky Mountain National Park as a wilderness area. This image shows Loch Vale, Taylor Peak, and the Sharkstooth on a windy winter day.

Painting by James Disney. Courtesy of James Disney.

Mary Sabin. Along with James Grafton Rogers, she was a key figure in the founding of the Colorado Mountain Club.

Courtesy of Colorado Mountain Club Archives.

She is a somewhat unwilling climber on the start, while I am always eager to get off. But when we once reach the top she is more enthusiastic than I. She gets down in good condition, but is tired for a few days afterward, while I am very tired that night but fresh the next day." Mary retired from teaching in 1931. (Florence earned her MD degree, becoming the first female professor at Johns Hopkins University and, later, the first female researcher at the Rockefeller Institute. She also was the first female member of the National Academy of Science.)[2]

Rogers, Mary Sabin, and the charter members of the Colorado Mountain Club typified the kind of people who had founded the Appalachian Mountain Club (1876); the Sierra Club (1892); the Mazamas (1894); and the Seattle Mountaineers (1906), originally part of the Mazamas. Most were well-educated, influential members in their communities. Enos Mills knew this, which is almost certainly why he wanted a mountain club formed: CMC members could provide powerful support for realizing his dream of establishing a national park in the Estes Park area.

Mills had likely sought out Rogers in particular because the two men already knew each other. According to Rogers, they first met in 1895, when Mills was 25 years old and Rogers was 12.

The two were very different people. They were initially friends, however, both dedicated to creating a national park. (But a few years after the club was formed, Mills turned on Rogers, as we discuss later.)

Mills came from a small town in Kansas, having been schooled through the eighth grade. He was sickly, later diagnosed as being wheat intolerant. At the age of 14, he headed west to Estes Park, where he stayed at the home of his uncle Elkanah Lamb and his family while working at various resorts. At 19, Mills had a chance meeting with John Muir, who became his mentor. Muir incited Mills not only to travel, to read, and to learn but also to work for the preservation of scenery, to polish his speaking and writing skills, and to interest the common man in nature—to become, essentially, its interpreter.

Well before 1910, Mills had become a staunch advocate for what eventually did become Rocky Mountain National Park. Although he'd written a few books, he was far better known nationally as a speaker, having presented more than 2,000 "forestry addresses" in addition to short talks about trees, birds, and nature.[3]

Rogers, whose parents were Canadian, was born in Denver. After graduating from Yale, he earned a law degree at the University of Denver. He then married Cora May Peabody, whose father, James, had been governor of Colorado from 1903 to 1905. (Gubernatorial terms were only two years at that time.) One of Rogers's law partners was Morrison Shafroth, whose father, John, had been governor and served as a US senator from 1913 to 1919.

Rogers wrote that Morrison Shafroth, as chair of the CMC's National Park Committee, may have been one of the club's most powerful benefactors, "always ready to travel to Washington with boxes of lantern slides and portfolios of photographs, in hopes of furthering the park cause."

In the summer of 1912, Chief Geographer Robert Marshall of the US Geological Survey (not to be confused with Bob Marshall, born in 1901, who worked for the Forest Service and was one of the founders of The Wilderness Society) took a vigorous six-day trip to examine the topography of the proposed park. He was impressed. In December, Marshall issued a glowing report on the area's scenery, enthusiastically endorsing the project.

With Marshall's go-ahead, one of the first orders of business became figuring out what land the national park would include. As

Enos Mills. Naturalist, innkeeper, and lecturer, the irascible Mills was a major force in the creation of Rocky Mountain National Park.

Courtesy of Colorado Mountain Club Archives.

Dawn at Streamside. Like so many other climbers, early members of the Colorado Mountain Club went on outings, often sleeping on bare ground in bedrolls without mattresses or tents.

Courtesy of Colorado Mountain Club Archives.

Rogers wrote: "Nobody had made public and familiar such essential elements as boundaries, acreage or property problems. There were no detailed maps except amateurish sketches, few, crude, and erroneous. In these matters the Club could contribute more familiarity and geographic knowledge than any agency in America. And it did. The Club drew the first outline of boundaries."

In 1905, on top of a mountain where Marshall was surveying, Rogers and Marshall encountered each other for the first time. "They sat and talked of many things, including Marshall's difficulties in determining

Women's Tug o' War. Throwing decorum to the winds, these hikers had enough energy left to test which group was the strongest and most determined in this early Colorado Mountain Club outing.

Courtesy of Colorado Mountain Club Archives.

the right names for mountains on the Bear Creek watershed." Rogers assisted Marshall in resolving these issues.

So, in 1913, when Marshall came to Denver, he sought out Rogers, and the two men strategized about the proposed park. Marshall, whom Rogers later called "very wise and helpful," said that Congress would be much more likely to approve the new park if its geographical features had names rather than blanks.[4]

To this end, in 1914, Rogers formed the CMC nomenclature committee, appointing Harriet Vaille as chair. Nearly 50 years later, she described the committee's mission: "As the Mountain Club campers of 1913 ranged the mountains and cañons, they were struck by the utter wildness and lack of human association in the region and they wondered if it would not be possible to recover some Indian memories and names to add interest for future

Puddle Jumper. Agnes Vaille, one of Colorado's most famous early mountaineers, practices a puddle jump at an early Colorado Mountain Club outing.

Courtesy of Colorado Mountain Club Archives.

Arapaho Elders. Harriet Vaille of the Colorado Mountain Club arranged for these tribal elders from the Wind River Reservation in Wyoming to come to Colorado to provide the Arapaho names for many geographic features in the new national park. From left, Tom Crispin, the interpreter; Sherman Sage; and Gun Griswold.

Courtesy Rocky Mountain National Park.

visitors to the hoped for national park. [The nomenclature committee's] big project was to bring some old Indians back to our mountains. Mr. Rogers asked Dr. Livingston Farrand, noted anthropologist, for guidance in this. Dr. Farrand was then the President of the University of Colorado and kindly met with the committee." He advised them to consult some northern Arapahos from the Wind River Reservation in Wyoming. Vaille went to Chicago's Newberry Library to research the Indians in the Rockies. Meanwhile, her friend, Edna Hendrie, went to Washington, D.C., where, "working through the kind offices of Senator Shafroth," the Commissioner of Indian Affairs wrote a letter of introduction to the superintendent of the Wind River Reservation requesting that he help the young women in every way he could. "This he certainly did," Vaille recalled.

Vaille and Hendrie interviewed Arapahos on the reservation, finally arranging for three of them to take the train to Colorado. They were Gun Griswold, at 73, the group's patriarch; Sherman Sage, 63, chief of police on the reservation; and Tom Crispin, 38, a fluent interpreter. In Longmont, the trio was met by two cars, one driven by the Hendrie chauffeur, and the other by Vaille's father, F. O., who insisted on driving his own vehicle. He also insisted that Gun Griswold sit beside him.

They stayed at Enos Mills's Longs Peak Inn. On July 16, the party set out on horseback. In addition to the Arapahos, the party consisted of Shep Husted, a superb mountain guide from Estes Park; Oliver Toll, Vaille's cousin, whom she chose as the group's leader and official recorder of information; and David Hawkins, a young tourist from the East and a CMC member. (Vaille did not join the party because it wasn't considered appropriate for respectable women to accompany an all-male group.)

The party rode to Grand Lake by one route and back to Longs Peak Inn by another, returning on July 28. As a result of Toll's meticulous notes, the group gained much knowledge of the region and its many Arapaho names, such as "Lumpy Ridge," the "Twin Owls," and the "Never Summer Range."

As Rogers remembered, "Marshall would not even print an advance sheet of the Longs Park [Peak] Quadrangle until we [the CMC] had named dozens of peaks, lakes and streams. We explored local history, gathered the lore of a party of Arapaho Indians, and borrowed names of clouds, minerals, miners, plants and birds to fill the vacancy."[5]

Taking the advice of Frederick Ross, the helpful and influential president of the Denver Chamber of Commerce, Rogers conducted extensive research and consulted with many people before he drafted a bill to present to Congress in February 1913. It went nowhere. For the next two years, Rogers persisted. Finally, after frustrating delays and revisions, his hard work paid off.

Hearings before the House Committee on Public Lands began on December 23, 1914. Oklahoma Congressman Scott Ferris, chairman, presided, while Colorado Congressman Edward T. Taylor guided testimony. Testifying for the bill on that date were retiring Colorado Governor Elias M. Ammons, Governor-elect George A. Carlson,

Nearing Passage. James Grafton Rogers, the first president of the Colorado Mountain Club, sought help from outdoor clubs such as the Seattle-based Mountaineers in his long campaign to create Rocky Mountain National Park.

Courtesy of Colorado Mountain Club Archives.

Dedicating the Park. Although President Woodrow Wilson signed the bill creating Rocky Mountain National Park into law on January 26, 1915, its official dedication in Horseshoe Park didn't take place until September 4, 1915.

Courtesy of Rocky Mountain National Park Archives.

Senator John F. Shafroth, and someone who had already given more than 300 lectures on the matter—Enos Mills.

Eventually, after a few minor amendments, the bill passed the Senate, and on January 26, 1915, President Woodrow Wilson signed it into law. Although reduced from the 700 square miles that Marshall had originally proposed, to 358.5 square miles, there was, at last, a Rocky Mountain National Park.[6]

Rocky Mountain National Park Map. Members of the Colorado Mountain Club had proposed many names for mountains and lakes in the park; the process of making those names official often took a year or more. As a result, the first official map of the park, issued in 1915, had few named features.

Courtesy of Colorado Mountain Club Archives.

Today the park is 415 square miles. Additions include Comanche Peak and Mirror Lake on the north; Deer Mountain, Gem Lake, Twin Sisters, and Lily Lake on the east; Ogallala Peak, St. Vrain Mountain, and several of the Hutcheson lakes on the south; and the high peaks of the Never Summer Range on the west.

As demonstrated by the quote that begins this chapter, Rogers was deeply affected by the experience. The process also changed Mills. Alexander Drummond, Mills's biographer, wrote: "The beginning of Enos's personal difficulties with Joe [Joe Mills, his younger brother] and others coincided with his rise to national fame." Mills even turned on Elkanah Lamb, with whom he'd traveled in Europe and from whom he'd purchased Longs Peak Inn, never acknowledging in print that Lamb was his uncle. Local residents of Tahosa Valley, many of whom had been former

Hagues Peak. At 13,560 feet, Hagues Peak is in the Mummy Range in Rocky Mountain National Park. Artist James Disney has twice been named the Artist in Residence in Rocky Mountain National Park and has climbed all 126 named peaks in the park.

Painting by James Disney. Courtesy of James Disney.

EARLY DEVELOPMENT

The park founded, the Colorado Mountain Club and its members continued to have a guiding role in its development for years to come. Particularly important in this effort was Roger Toll, another founder of the club. A civil engineer by profession and an avid climber, Toll had a chance meeting with Steven Mather, the first head of the National Park Service, while on a trip to Hawaii. That meeting culminated in Toll's appointment first, in 1917, as superintendent of Mount Rainier National Park and two years later as superintendent of Rocky Mountain National Park.

Roger Toll. Seen here probably in Mount Rainier National Park measuring snow depth, Toll was one of the most influential superintendents of Rocky Mountain National Park.
Courtesy of Rocky Mountain National Park Archives.

Toll used the reports of CMC members to compile a book, edited by Robert Sterling Yard and published by the Government Printing Office in 1919, titled *Mountaineering in the Rocky Mountain National Park*. It manifested his views of the outdoors. He wrote in the foreword: "Mountaineering, in its broader sense, promotes the health and strength of the body, it teaches self-reliance, determination, presence of mind, necessity for individual thought and action, pride of accomplishment, fearlessness, endurance, helpful cooperation, loyalty, patriotism, the love of an unselfish freedom, and many other qualities that make for sturdy manhood and womanhood."

Hallett Glacier Grotto. This image, made from a hand-tinted lantern slide, depicts a party of climbers from the Colorado Mountain Club exploring a grotto in what is now known as Rowe Glacier. It is doubtful that the grotto still exists.
Photograph by C. F. Reed.
Courtesy of the Colorado Historical Society.

Under Toll's leadership, the park expanded. It acquired the Never Summer Range and developed the Bear Lake Road, North Longs Peak Trail, North Inlet Trail, and Lawn Lake Trail. He also supervised the construction of the Vaille Shelter, near the Keyhole on Longs Peak, as a memorial to his cousin Agnes Vaille, considered by many to be Colorado's most famous woman climber of that era, who had died nearby after a winter ascent of the east face of the mountain. Toll became the first person to climb the 50 highest peaks in the park. And his farsighted persistence led to the creation of Trail Ridge Road, the highest continuously paved road in the United States, which was completed by his successor, Edmund Rogers, another charter member of the Colorado Mountain Club, after Toll left his post with the park in 1929 to become superintendent of Yellowstone National Park.

Although his life was cut short by an automobile crash in 1936, he left an indelible imprint. To honor Toll, the federal government changed the name of a Colorado peak known as Paiute Horn to Mount Toll, which is now part of the Indian Peaks Wilderness Area. Also erected in his honor is a bronze plaque and mountain index, known as the Toll Memorial, on a high point near Trail Ridge Road. And in Texas, the National Park Service named a peak Toll Mountain to honor the man, whose evaluation had been instrumental in creating Big Bend National Park.

While many have attributed the creation and development of Rocky Mountain National Park to one individual, Enos Mills, dozens of people and organizations were responsible for it. Both Mills and James Grafton Rogers were giants in the movement to create the park, and Roger Toll was perhaps its most important early superintendent. All the players who launched the effort are gone now, and many details of the story have been lost. But what is left are their legacies, among them Rocky Mountain National Park and the Colorado Mountain Club.

supporters of Mills, proposed changing the name to Elkanah Valley. Mills, who first saw the valley 10 years after Lamb had homesteaded there, objected strenuously. Harriet Vaille, secretary of the Colorado Geographical Board, dutifully recorded the gist of a conversation the two had: "Mr. Mills, for personal reasons, very much resented the name Elkanah, saying that the name had no particular connections with the valley."

Historian Carl Abbott put it more harshly: "Despite his willingness to invest his reputation as a nature writer in the advocacy of conservation and national parks, something in his personality forced him to destroy the personal and professional relationships that he had developed and that were necessary for effectiveness. He shunned compromise, alienated potential allies, and used up friends like typewriter ribbons, good for one project but discarded before the next."

Mills's reputation declined. However, 50 years after the Rocky Mountain National Park's creation, Rogers wrote of Mills: "His science seems a little extravagant as I look over his volumes today and some of his tales are borrowed, but in the mass his message is authentic. Mills quarreled with many people and in later years was hostile to the Mountain Club, to the National Park and to me, but my admiration and even affection have not faded."

Regardless of the individual personalities involved, it is clear that the CMC provided the impetus for the park's creation. In 1965, a park superintendent said, "Had it not been for the Colorado Mountain Club, there would not be a Rocky Mountain National Park." And Roger Toll wrote: "The part played by the Colorado Mountain Club in the establishment of the Park is evidenced by the fact that [two of its early] superintendents, Roger W. Toll and Edmund B. Rogers, were drawn and appointed from its active membership and not from the Washington bureaucracy.[7]

Moraine Park. A charter member of the Colorado Mountain Club, Charles Partridge Adams
found Rocky Mountain National Park an inspiration for many of his works.

Painting by Charles Partridge Adams, c. 1900.
Courtesy of Denver Art Museum. Collection from various donors by exchange. 1996.8

Mount Massive. The shoulders of Colorado's second highest peak loom over the landscape in the heart of the Mount Massive Wilderness Area.

Photograph by Christopher J. Case. Courtesy of Christopher J. Case.

CHAPTER 2

REACHING HIGHER

WALTER R. BORNEMAN

The first piece of rope I remember using in the mountains was that summer [1920] in the San Juans. The rope was just something to hang on—sort of a handhold—climbing some of the steeper snowbanks. If someone slipped in line, the rest of us would hold the rope.... That was the first way we used ropes.
—CARL BLAUROCK

Early goals for climbing mountains in Colorado tended to have a practical, work-related aspect. Explorers sought answers to geographic riddles; prospectors searched for ore outcrops; surveyors mapped a maze of peaks and valleys. Recreational climbs, when they occurred, were most often via easy routes up a few celebrity peaks. These became the emotional and physical high points on a budding Colorado tourist circuit. Mining vagabond Dick Irwin constructed a horse trail up Grays Peak and had tourists riding to the top in the late 1860s. A trail, a carriage road, a cog railway, and finally an auto road reached the summit of Pikes Peak. Climbing a difficult peak "just for fun" was definitely the exception.

William S. Cooper and John V. Hubbard were exceptions by any measure. Cooper was born in Detroit in 1884. At the age of 20, he spent a summer in far-off Colorado and got his first taste of mountaineering on an ascent of Longs Peak. His guide was Enos Mills, then in the early years of his guiding

Pioneer Climbers. William S. Cooper and John V. Hubbard were among Colorado's first recreational mountaineers.

Courtesy of Colorado Mountain Club Archives.

service. Cooper was hooked, and after graduating from Alma College in Michigan, he returned to Colorado in the summer of 1906. There, he met Hubbard, a Colorado School of Mines graduate, who was employed at Mills's Longs Peak Inn.

After traipsing around the Estes Park area with Hubbard, Cooper made a solo visit to mountains that Mills had urged him to see. Taking the narrow gauge train to Silverton deep in the San Juan Mountains, Cooper hiked up Kendall Mountain east of town and was staggered by the view. To the south, the sweeping north faces of Arrow, Vestal, and the Trinity peaks of the Grenadier Range rose in rugged symmetry. Beyond, the spire of Pigeon Peak towered some 5,700 feet above the canyon of the Animas River and stood starkly apart from its pointy Needle Mountain neighbors. "Here were mountains," Cooper later wrote, "that I must see again, and at the earliest opportunity: the whole San Juan country, the Needle Mountains in particular, and, first of all, Pigeon Peak."

His earliest opportunity proved to be the summer of 1908, and Cooper's logical companion was kindred soul John Hubbard. On July 11, in the face of an approaching thunderstorm, the duo reached the 13,972-foot summit of Pigeon Peak. All evidence suggested that it was a first ascent. Even a century later, a tough approach and an imposing summit block make Pigeon Peak a demanding climb.

From Pigeon's summit, the rest of their itinerary was plainly visible. Four days later, Cooper and Hubbard crossed into the beautiful valley of turquoise-blue Balsam Lake and made first ascents of 13,864-foot Vestal Peak and 13,803-foot Arrow Peak, the latter via a moderately difficult rock-climbing route on the mountain's south face. As William M. Bueler, acknowledged as the dean of Colorado's mountaineering historians, aptly noted, "Many Colorado climbers would rate these three among the ten most impressive mountains in the state."

San Juan Challenge. The blocky monolith of 13,972-foot Pigeon Peak dominates the view south of Silverton.

Photograph by David Anschicks. Courtesy of David Anschicks.

Wham Ridge. Located on the north side of Vestal Peak, with the similarly shaped north buttress of West Trinity Peak in the distance, Wham Ridge presents some of Colorado's more challenging summit routes.

Photograph by David Anschicks. Courtesy of David Anschicks.

Cooper went on to earn a PhD from the University of Chicago and become one of the leading specialists in plant succession following glacial retreat. His studies as a botany professor at the University of Minnesota led him to Alaska's Glacier Bay, where he was instrumental in the establishment of Glacier Bay National Monument, now a national park. But, ironically, this lover of the high peaks who clearly sought difficult climbs for the fun of it, was unable to climb seriously after his 1908 romp through Colorado. Returning to Detroit that fall, Cooper complained of chest pains and dizziness. A doctor told him that he had strained his heart during the exertion of the previous summer and that he should avoid such activity in the future. The diagnosis is open to doubt, but Cooper took the doctor's advice—for another 70 years until he died at the age of 94 in Boulder, Colorado, not far from his first mountain.[1]

Climbing mountains always took on a more serious air when the possibility of a first ascent was at stake. Explorers, prospectors, and surveyors were the first to reach the summits of most of Colorado's 14,000-foot peaks, commonly known as Fourteeners. Earlier Native American first ascents almost certainly occurred. Still, by 1916, there were three summits among Colorado's Fourteeners that were generally accepted to be untouched. They lay in the long, narrow northern section of the Sangre de Cristo Range, peaks known from the valleys by Spanish explorers as early as the 1700s but still unmapped two centuries later.

Adding to the mystery of what really lay up there was the fact that the names of these three summits seemed to shift depending on who was telling the story. Suffice it to say, here was a challenge for mountaineers. Among those equal to the task was Albert R. Ellingwood, who taught political science at his undergraduate alma mater, Colorado College. A stint of climbing in Europe while a Rhodes scholar at Oxford University had sharpened both his academic skills and his technical abilities as a rock climber. The use of a rope in any manner of mountaineering was rare in the United States, but while abroad, Ellingwood learned the basic techniques of belaying for protection that European climbers were using in the Alps.

Armed with that experience, Ellingwood's party of eight—himself and seven women—set off for the Crestones, "fed in part," in Ellingwood's words, "by tales of peaks unclimbed and peaks unclimbable." They made their first camp above the lush meadows of the Willow Creek valley "in one of the prettiest campsites I have seen in Colorado," according to Ellingwood. The first task was to ascend Kit Carson Peak, a relatively easy scramble via its northwest ridge. Climbing over the 14,081-foot northwest sub-peak that is now known as Challenger Point, the group discovered the "sloping ledge with the width of a boulevard" that is the key when gaining the upper slopes from the west.

With Kit Carson's summit won, "the more energetic of the party" took two days of rations and set up a camp in the Spanish Creek drainage from which to test "the unclimbability of the Crestones." Although Ellingwood later bemoaned the late start, it was a leisurely 8:10 a.m. on July 24, 1916, before Ellingwood, Eleanor Davis, Frances "Bee" Rogers, and Jo Deutchbein bashed their way through "a tedious patch of willows" and started up Crestone Peak's northeast arête from near the Crestone–Humboldt saddle.

Ready for the Trail. Albert R. Ellingwood and seven women mountaineers prepare to depart to climb the Crestones in 1916.

Courtesy of Colorado Mountain Club Archives.

Signing the Summit Register.
Albert R. Ellingwood, Barton Hoag, and Eleanor
Davis (left to right) enjoy another successful outing
in the High Country.

Courtesy of Colorado Mountain Club Archives.

Crestone Peak (left) and the Crestone Needle.
After Albert R. Ellingwood and Eleanor Davis reached
the summits of Crestone Peak and Crestone Needle
on July 24, 1916, the myth of the "unclimbability"
of the Crestones was laid to rest.

Photograph by Dave Cooper. Courtesy of Dave Cooper.

As the route steepened, Ellingwood broke out the rope and belayed where prudence dictated. After zigzagging from one side of the arête to the other, the group traversed west and finally emerged from the top of the prominent north couloir between the peak's twin summits. They turned right and reached the higher western summit just before 1:00 p.m. Ellingwood calculated erroneously that the eastern summit was higher, and the foursome climbed it as well, building cairns on both points. Now, there was but one summit to go.

Across a half-mile ridge of spires, Crestone Needle beckoned. Deutchbein and Rogers opted to descend the south couloir and return to camp by circling west around Crestone Peak, but Ellingwood and Davis continued to climb over and around "the gendarmes that stood up like Cleopatra's Needle on the east." At last, the two were at the base of the conglomerate-studded northwest wall just below the Crestone Needle summit. It is likely that Ellingwood climbed it first and then belayed Davis to the top. There were no longer any unclimbed Fourteeners in Colorado.

It is interesting to speculate on Ellingwood's choice of a descent route. Those who have been on these peaks know that precise directions are impossible among the juxtaposition of numerous ribs and gullies. But descend they did, apparently via much of today's standard route to the Crestone Needle–Broken Hand saddle. From here, with the sun sinking, Ellingwood and Davis chose to turn east to descend to South Colony Lakes and return to their camp via the Crestone–Humboldt saddle. Wind blew out their candle lantern long before they wearily stumbled upon their tents just before midnight.[2]

But that is not quite the whole story. Ellingwood may have turned east to circle the Crestone Needle because his eyes were drawn to a line that appeared to lead straight up from South Colony Lakes to the

The Crestone Group. Looming on the horizon are the famous peaks of the Crestone group: at left, the long ridge of Challenger Point (named for the tragic space shuttle *Challenger*), the pyramid-like summit of Kit Carson Peak, Kit Carson Observation Point, and several sub-peaks in the center; at right center, Crestone Peak; at far right, Crestone Needle.

Photograph by Dave Cooper. Courtesy of Dave Cooper.

summit. He never forgot the sight. It took him nine years, but in August 1925, Ellingwood returned with Marian Warner, Stephen H. Hart, and the nimble Eleanor Davis.

Standing on a knoll near the lakes, the quartet thought that the lower 1,500 feet looked doable, but voiced grave doubts about what happened when the line grew more vertical and even appeared to be

A Stitch in Time. Early climbing gear—and repairs to same—were often ad hoc. Note the hobnail boots, the climber perched over the log, and the delicate nature of this repair to torn pants.

Courtesy of Colorado Mountain Club Archives.

Food for Three Weeks. In the 1930s, climbers like the Melzers did not have the luxury of freeze-dried food, but by gosh, this stuff still looked good.

Courtesy of Melzer Collection.

NAILING YOUR BOOTS

You can tell a lot about a mountaineer by the look of his or her boots. Long before Vibram soles, Lowas, or Five Tens, a pattern of hobnails snugly nailed into soles meant you were ready for the high peaks. Serious climbers added edging nails around the perimeter. About an inch long with a big head, malleable edging nails were driven through the sole from the bottom just outside the welt and then bent over on the outside and clinched under the nail's head. "A keg of nice sharp Swiss edging nails is now on tap at the Club room," *Trail & Timberline* reported in June 1923. "They are better than eyebrows when it comes to clinging on cliffs, and will make a pair of soles last at least three times as long as the ordinary hobs alone."

overhanging in one place. Surmounting the initial section, the team huddled beneath "one under-sized poncho, sitting mostly on imagination," remembered Ellingwood.

They ate lunch as a pounding hailstorm blanketed their contemplated route with pea-sized ball bearings of hail that made every foothold suspect and quickly numbed fingers seeking the security of a safe hold. Twice, Ellingwood led difficult cracks without knowing if suitable belay stances waited above. Both times, they did, and after spending four hours climbing 400 feet of cold, wet rock, the party emerged on Crestone Needle's summit ridge less than 100 feet from the summit cairn.

"No one," Ellingwood later wrote, "will ever run up the Needle's east arête just to get up an appetite for breakfast. [But] it is a first-class climb . . . furnishing enough thrills and technical difficulties and sensational views to satisfy the most sophisticated cragsman." A climb of Ellingwood Arête was not repeated until Bob Ormes led it in 1937, three years after Ellingwood's untimely death at the age of 37.[3] (By contrast, Eleanor Davis [later Eleanor Davis Ehrman] lived to a spry 107, dying in 1994.)

Throughout the 1930s, the Colorado Mountain Club continued to lead numerous summer outings and weekend climbing trips around the state. Participants in the trips visited old favorites and explored new areas, such as those encountered during the 1935 outing in the Gore Range that made the first known ascents of at least seven of the range's peaks.

The United States was mired in the Great Depression at this time, and recreation was a welcome escape. Frequently, climbing as recreation was a family affair. Carl Melzer and his young son, Bob, took family adventures to the extreme in 1936, when, along with 19-year-old Julius Johnson, they hiked the length of Colorado's Continental Divide from the Wyoming border to New Mexico. Grace Melzer, Carl's wife, served as the chief supply officer. Driving a 1936 Chevrolet, she met her husband and son at pre-arranged spots atop 16 mountain passes to restock their provisions and assess their generally wet condition from an unusually rainy summer.

The following year, when Bob Melzer was all of nine, the father-and-son duo determined to climb Colorado's Fourteeners—then a list of 51. The task took Carl and Bob 69 days and covered 4,000 miles, including a week's respite in Denver while Bob endured a bout of tonsillitis. The summer's adventure cost a total of $187. Carl, who was a Breckenridge

Satisfaction. Carl Melzer's mountaineering took him to the summit of Gannett Peak in the Wind River Mountains of Wyoming in 1943.

Courtesy of Melzer Collection.

DATE: *August 26, 1920*

MOUNTAIN: *Lizard Head Peak*

CLIMBERS: *Albert R. Ellingwood and Barton Hoag*

EVENT: *First ascent of 350-foot volcanic plug two miles east of Mount Wilson*

SIGNIFICANCE: *Given the steepness and crumbly nature of the rock, it was likely the hardest rock climb achieved to date in Colorado. The descent proved more terrifying than the ascent. After being hit by falling rocks, Ellingwood was forced to re-climb a pitch twice in an attempt to dislodge the rappel rope before "regretfully saying goodbye to the rope that had served me well for five good seasons."*

Lizard Head. First climbed by Albert R. Ellingwood and Barton Hoag, the crumbling pinnacle of Lizard Head presented an imposing challenge to early mountaineers. This famous ascent pushed Colorado climbing standards to new heights.

Courtesy of Colorado Mountain Club Archives.

high school teacher at the time, explained, "It had to be cheap fun or a school-teacher could not do it." By climbing the 51 peaks, the Melzers became only the fifth and sixth persons to climb all the Fourteeners.

After such ambitious travels, another obvious goal presented itself: The Melzers decided to become the first to climb all the 14,000-foot peaks in the contiguous 48 states. This meant that they would need to climb 13 additional peaks located in California and one, Mount Rainier, in Washington. In the summer of 1939, Carl Blaurock and Elwyn Arps joined the Melzers for some of the climbs. The adults were all members of the Colorado Mountain Club, but young Bob complained, "They wouldn't let me in; I'm not big enough." After their climbing swing through California, father and son achieved their goal by reaching the summit of Mount Rainier.

Carl Melzer later earned a PhD from the University of California and taught at the University of Denver. Bob became a prominent Denver surgeon. Any doubt as to whether he truly enjoyed those summer rambles as a youngster was dispelled, as Bob spent a lifetime trekking in mountains all over the world. And his son, Tom, along with Tom's wife, Judy, repeated Bob's first adventure by walking the Colorado portion of the Continental Divide Trail in 1976.[4]

Longs Peak East Face Routes. Longs is one of the outstanding climber's peaks in North America. Its east face is 1,675 feet, with a 975-foot cliff, the Diamond, looming entirely above 13,100 feet. The first legendary ascent routes displayed include Alexanders Chimney of 1922, which was the first ascent of the east face; Stettners Ledges, 1927; the North Chimney, 1924; the Second or Kieners Chimney, 1936; Notch Couloir, 1922; Broadway Cutoff, 1926; and The Cables—put up in 1925 but removed in 1973. Today, Longs' east face has more climbing routes—in excess of 75—than any other major mountain in North America.

Courtesy of Denver Public Library.

One Born Every Minute. Carl Blaurock stood on his head after reaching the summit of every Fourteener he climbed. "I wanted my feet higher on the mountain than anybody else," he explained.

Courtesy of Colorado Mountain Club Archives.

OTHER LUMINARY COLORADO CLIMBERS

Carl Blaurock (1894–1993). Carl Blaurock was the quintessential mountaineer. From his first climb of Pikes Peak in 1909 to his death just shy of 99 in 1993, Carl's love of mountains was second only to his love for his wife of 65 years, Louise, whom he met on the 1925 CMC outing. Short and wiry in his youth, Carl always led the way, from first ascents with Albert R. Ellingwood in Wyoming's Wind River Range to his final climb of Notch Mountain at the age of 79 to commemorate the centennial of William Henry Jackson's historic photograph of Mount of the Holy Cross. Carl's prose graced numerous *Trail & Timberline* issues, and he was an accomplished photographer. He was especially pleased when, 60 years after his first Wind River travels, the University of Wyoming asked for his photographs from that trip—still meticulously labeled in Carl's fashion—to compare recent changes in glaciers.

DATE: September 14, 1927

MOUNTAIN: Longs Peak, east face/
Stettners Ledges

CLIMBERS: Joe Stettner and Paul Stettner

EVENT: Most direct route to date on east face of
Longs Peak

SIGNIFICANCE: Recent immigrants from Germany,
the Stettner brothers were well versed in
roped climbing, although they had to rely on
120 feet of hemp rope purchased at the
general store in nearby Estes Park. When Joe
voiced reservations "about some ice places,"
younger brother Paul—all of 21—told him,
"We can worry about that when we get
there." Working up a series of cracks and
ledges leading to Broadway, the Stettners
pioneered a route that remained a Colorado
test piece until after World War II.

Heading to Colorado. Gasoline was cheap
when the Stettner brothers, Joe and Paul, rode
motorcycles across the plains from Chicago to
climb the east face of Longs Peak via the route
that became known as Stettners Ledges.

Courtesy of Colorado Mountain Club Archives.

DATE: *September 2, 1929*

MOUNTAIN: *Lone Eagle Peak*

CLIMBERS: *Carl Blaurock, William Ervin, and Stephen H. Hart*

EVENT: *First ascent of Lone Eagle Peak (then known as Lindbergh Peak)*

SIGNIFICANCE: *This airy summit is not the high point, but the end of a long ridge towering over Crater Lake in the Indian Peaks. The first-ascent climbers were all stalwart members of the Colorado Mountain Club. While the route was not particularly difficult by later standards, photographs of the trio scooting along the exposed summit ridge while roped together caused a sensation in the CMC clubrooms. It showed that Colorado climbers were indeed seeking out harder and harder climbs.*[5]

Lone Eagle Peak. Originally known as Lindbergh Peak, this spire took the name Lone Eagle Peak following the sobriquet of the famed aviator Charles Lindbergh, the first person to fly solo across the Atlantic Ocean.

Courtesy of Colorado Mountain Club Archives.

OTHER LUMINARY COLORADO CLIMBERS

Mary Cronin (1893–1982). Mary Cronin was the fourth person and first woman to climb all of Colorado's 14,000-foot peaks. A Colorado Mountain Club member since 1921, Mary completed the Fourteener list (then 51 peaks) after reaching the summits of Mount Belford and Mount Oxford on September 2, 1934. Three years later, Cronin and Carl Blaurock led a CMC party on a difficult route on Blanca Peak's north face. This was one of her last climbs, as her work for Western Union soon took her to Omaha and Dallas, although she remained a CMC member for 61 years. When Mary Cronin died in Port Angeles, Washington, memorials were directed to the Colorado Mountain Club, and she was buried in Denver's Fairmount Cemetery not far from Carl Blaurock and Bill Ervin.[6]

Mary Cronin on Columbine Pass. A friend and climbing partner of Carl Blaurock, Cronin became the first woman to climb all of Colorado's then-known 14,000-foot peaks.

Courtesy of Colorado Mountain Club Archives.

Lupine and the Sneffels Range. Flowers gracing the high
alpine slopes of the Rockies have long attracted climbers.
Photograph by Glenn Randall. Courtesy of Glenn Randall.

CHAPTER 3

CLIMBING HARDER

WALTER R. BORNEMAN

I should find it hard to put into words to you tonight what it has meant to me over the years to slip off on a mountain path for an hour when I needed to or how often I've worked out the tangles and problems of life as I plodded along through the quiet of a high pine forest.

—BETSY COWLES PARTRIDGE

World War II interrupted idyllic summers in the Rockies, but Colorado's mountains also provided respite from the war effort. The CMC's 1942 outing had been planned for the favorite peaks and valleys of the Needle Mountains, but rationing forced a rescheduling to the needles of the Gore Range—much closer to Denver. As Carl Melzer reported in *Trail & Timberline*, "Our tires still had 20 miles left in them and Eddie at the filling station said we were good for 15 gallons of gas."

After the war, pushing the limits of technical rock climbing took on renewed energy and centered on the Flatirons west of Boulder. Ascents of the First and Third Flatirons had long been local staples, but now climbers pushed harder routes on those and other formations. These included the first ascent of The Matron in 1948 by Bill Eubanks, Brad Vandiver, and Stan Black and pioneering routes on the West Overhang and the East Ridge routes of The Maiden in 1953 by Dale Johnson, Dave Robertson, Phil Robertson, and Cary Huston.[1]

Descending The Maiden. Roy and Alice Holubar chose The Maiden above Boulder to dramatize the cover of their 1963/1964 mountaineering catalog. Here, Wes Horner is doing a 110-foot free rappel off The Maiden in the late 1940s. The image was a hallmark for Holubar Mountaineering Ltd., until its sale to Jim Kack and later Johnson & Johnson and ultimately The North Face.

Photograph by Roy Holubar. Courtesy of Janet N. and David Robertson.

Search and Rescue. Until after World War II, there were no mountain rescue organizations. The growing popularity of mountaineering in the postwar years changed that. With more people climbing harder mountains and using more difficult routes, search and rescue operations had to keep pace with the increasingly higher standards of mountaineering.

Photograph by Tom Hornbein. Courtesy of Tom Hornbein.

Pushing the limits meant that mountain safety and rescue techniques also had to evolve. Peppered with veterans of the 10th Mountain Division, the Rocky Mountain Rescue Group was started in Boulder in 1947. Working with rudimentary ropes and slings, the group developed big-wall litter evacuation techniques and soon became one of the West's premier mountain rescue units. Early leaders included Tom Hornbein, who, along with Willi Unsoeld, would go on to make the first ascent of the West Ridge of Everest. For more casual enthusiasts, the Denver and Boulder groups of the CMC started formal climbing schools in 1947 with the requirement that beginning students had to have a good pair of tennis shoes, an 80- or 120-foot nylon or manila rope, and adequate clothing.[2]

The Dove. Born in Loveland, Colorado, in 1939, self-taught artist James Disney climbed many of the subjects he painted, including the West Rib route on Denali, all the Fourteeners, and the 126 named summits in Rocky Mountain National Park. This image captures the evening light on the north face of Longs Peak as seen from the Boulderfield. The large snowfield at the base of the face is called the Dove.

Painting by James Disney. Courtesy of James Disney.

As rock-climbing and mountain-rescue techniques were refined during the 1950s, the National Park Service decreed that some routes under its jurisdiction were simply too dangerous to climb. The most famous prohibition on climbing—perhaps because it was applied to one of the most coveted of unclimbed routes—was the smooth upper wall of Longs Peak's east face, that territory known as the Diamond. Decades later, many climbers ascended this face by numerous variations, but in 1960, just the thought of one route up it was enough to set pulses racing.

In California, the granite-walled valley of Yosemite was also part of a national park. Although the first ascent of the Nose route on El Capitan in 1958 was initially described as "stunt and daring trick climbing," this attitude quickly changed as ever-higher skill levels were

Dancing on Rock. Paige Claassen, with chalk in pouch, takes the lead on Genesis, a near-vertical slab of rock in Eldorado Canyon, south of Boulder. Challenging pitches shooting up dramatically off the trails below make Eldorado Canyon a mecca for climbers worldwide.

Photograph by Andy Mann. Courtesy of Andy Mann.

attained. In Colorado, these were exemplified by Ray Northcutt and Layton Kor's 1959 climb of the Diagonal on the east face of Longs below Broadway. In the summer of 1960, the Park Service suddenly reversed itself and permitted parties on the Diamond as long as they could show the required competence *and* provide a qualified support team to go to their rescue in the event of a problem.

When this new policy lifted the climbing ban on the Diamond, Northcutt, Kor, and other Colorado climbers were not readily available. Sensing a grand opportunity, two Yosemite veterans, a mathematician named David Rearick and a schoolteacher named Robert Kamps, scurried from California to Colorado. After repeating Northcutt and Kor's climb of the Diagonal, they proceeded to haul their gear up the North Chimney to Broadway at the base of the Diamond. A steady drizzle convinced them to forgo a bivouac on the ledge and return to the Chasm Lake shelter for one last night of relative comfort. Meanwhile, the towering wall above them remained veiled in clouds and laced with running water, which did nothing for their morale.

But as frequently happens in the mountains, dawn brought windy, clear skies, and after the two climbers ascended fixed lines to Broadway, Rearick led off on the first pitch of the Diamond. Kamps took the second pitch and encountered an overhanging roof that he surmounted by placing two direct-aid pitons. Above the fourth pitch, a threatening thunderstorm, typical of Longs, forced them to retreat to a bivouac on Broadway to avoid getting soaked. The storm blew itself out without much rain, and the two climbers "spent the evening eating salami, raisins and candy, and watching a spectacular lightning display out over the Great Plains."

Early the next morning, Rearick and Kamps re-climbed their ropes to the previous day's high point. Water now fell on them not from clouds, but from a waterfall cascading downward from a high ice block. They soon climbed behind the waterfall—proving that the face was indeed overhanging—and banged pitons into a narrow crack. The face continued to overhang to the point that their haul bags of gear came up behind them without touching the rock.

Their second night on the route was spent on a surface that was neither as wide nor as comfortable as their bivouac on Broadway. A two-foot ledge had to suffice. Rearick sat in a cross-legged position all night, while Kamps managed to recline partially. Climbing again on the third day, they encountered the blocks of ice in the summit chimney that spawned the long waterfall, and then finally forced their way to the summit shortly after noon on August 3, 1960. Kamps's wife, Bonnie, and several newspaper reporters, who had come up the regular north face cables route, greeted them.

As Rearick later wrote, "The extensive newspaper coverage of our climb, and the dizzy aftermath of parades, banquets and television appearances, showed the enthusiasm of Coloradans for mountain-climbing and confirmed the exalted reputation of the Diamond." In truth, some local Colorado climbers were miffed that these Californians had "stolen" their local climb, but the exchange of climbers between the Diamond on Longs Peak and the big walls of Yosemite encouraged competition, shared techniques and innovations, and greatly sped the development of the sport. As evidence of that, three years later, Californian Royal Robbins and Coloradan Layton Kor teamed up to make the second ascent of the Diamond in a single day.[3]

Colorado Mountain Club climbers took their skills to mountains throughout the world. Alaska legend Bradford Washburn got credit for pioneering the West Buttress route on Denali (Mount McKinley) in 1951, but few remember that Washburn actually joined a Colorado

Ray Northcutt on Flagstaff Mountain in the 1950s. Ray Northcutt was one of the first in Colorado to actively engage in free climbing as an end in itself.

Photograph by Ron Foreman. Courtesy of Ray Northcutt.

Glenn Porzak on Makalu. He became a respected expert on water law while developing a second career as a world-class mountaineer.

Photograph by Chris Pizzo. Courtesy of Glenn Porzak.

Gary Neptune on Gasherbrum II. He successfully combined sport and business with his climbing and Neptune Mountaineering in Boulder.

Photograph courtesy of Gary Neptune.

Mountain Club expedition led by Henry Buchtel and Mel Griffiths. CMC member Al Auten was instrumental in supporting Tom Hornbein and Willi Unsoeld's West Ridge of Everest ascent in 1963, while Dick Pownall climbed high on the South Col route.

Glenn Porzak and Gary Neptune took the CMC banner to the summit of Makalu in the Himalayas together in 1987 and individually reached the summit of Everest on other expeditions. Porzak's "Seven Summits" quest started on South America's Aconcagua in 1974 and ended with Carstensz Pyramid in Indonesia in 1994. Neptune also climbed at locations around the world, but he may be best known for Neptune Mountaineering, a Boulder outdoor retailer in operation since 1973, where no piece of gear is too specialized and the salesperson has likely recently used it—probably under Neptune's supervision. Meanwhile, the Colorado Mountain Club's High Altitude Mountaineering Section has led adventure expeditions to every continent.

One of the most memorable CMC outings occurred in 1964, when Dale and Julie Johnson of the Boulder Group led 48 participants on a two-month trip around the Alps. They piled into Volkswagen buses and divided into A hikers for easy hikes and cultural trips, B hikers for moderate outings, and C climbers for the big peaks and technical climbs. The C climbers accomplished a dream list of ascents that included the Matterhorn, the Breithorn, Civetta, the Marmolada, the Jungfrau, and Mount Blanc. Perhaps the most amazing aspect of the two-month trip was that it was accomplished for $800 per person, including airfare.

But to many Colorado mountaineers, their own backyard was still the best. Climbers of every generation tended to bemoan "the good old days"—fewer people, less traveled trails, more unclimbed peaks, and just more open spaces. But many challenges were yet to be found—some in unlikely places.

The Matterhorn High above the Breithorn Hut. Many American mountaineers have trained in Colorado to climb Europe's most famous mountain along with other peaks all over the world. Hut systems as extensive as those of Europe are the envy of the rest of the world.

Photograph by Roger Fuehrer. Courtesy of Roger Fuehrer.

Mike Caldwell was not the best climber in the world, but he held the distinction of being the teacher of arguably the best climber in the world—by no small coincidence, his son, Tommy. Growing up in Estes Park, Colorado, within sight of Longs Peak, Tommy Caldwell climbed the Diamond with his dad when he was 12 years old. As was the case with young Bob Melzer, there was never any question that he was climbing mountains for his own passion rather than just to satisfy paternal urgings. Tommy followed this passion on five continents and along the way pioneered numerous 5.14 climbs and one 5.15 sport climb. By 2010, he had free climbed more routes on El Capitan than anyone (11), five of them first ascents. But Estes Park and Colorado were still home.

In the summer of 2008, Mike Caldwell was hiking a peak in Rocky Mountain National Park when he spied a slender pinnacle some 300 feet high that from most angles blended into the rock of the neighboring mountain. Six air miles away nearly 3 million tourists a year visited Bear Lake, but here was new ground to be explored. Mike told Tommy about the spire and together they made what appeared to be a first ascent. And, like so many adventurers over a century of Colorado mountaineering, they did it for the fun of it.

The Caldwells on the Diamond. The diverse routes and challenges of Longs Peak have always attracted climbers of all ages and abilities. Here, Tommy Caldwell and his dad, Mike, pause for a break on Tommy's first ascent of the Diamond.

Courtesy of Tommy Caldwell.

DATE: *August 9–10, 1947*

MOUNTAIN: *Monitor Peak—east face*

CLIMBERS: *Joe Stettner, John Speck, and Jack Fralick*

EVENT: *First ascent of the 1,200-foot east face of Monitor Peak, Needle Mountains*

SIGNIFICANCE: *Twenty years after his climb of Stettner's Ledges, Joe Stettner led his rope mates up the most sustained rock climb achieved to date in Colorado, subsequently rated 5.8. It required a frosty bivouac and got harder as the climb progressed. Because the wall was at the head of seldom-visited Ruby Creek, the climb was not repeated for 21 years. At the time, however, it pushed the limits for postwar big-wall climbing that was about to refocus on Longs Peak.*

After the Climb. Joe Stettner hugs John Speck (left) and Jack Fralick after the first ascent of the east face of Monitor Peak deep in the San Juan Mountains.

Courtesy of Colorado Mountain Club Archives.

DATE: April 29—May 3, 1972

MOUNTAIN: Black Canyon of the Gunnison—the Painted Wall

CLIMBERS: Bill E. Forrest and Kris Walker

EVENT: First ascent of the tallest vertical wall in Colorado

SIGNIFICANCE: Gear aficionado and big-wall climber Bill E. Forrest called this 5.11 climb of the 2,600-foot Painted Wall his "most extreme rock climb." For five days, he and Kris Walker endured tiny bivouac ledges and climbed through 26 pitches. Loose rock in all the wrong places added to the problems. Pitch 24 took Forrest five and one-half hours to lead in what he called "an ultimate physical and technical challenge where success was imperative but doubtful." Impressive for 1972, the technical difficulty and sustained climbing created a stir among climbers throughout the United States. As Forrest wrote afterward, "We knew the secrets of the Painted Wall, we knew each other, and we were happy."[4]

The Painted Wall. The challenges presented by the so-called Painted Wall in the Black Canyon of the Gunnison led Bill E. Forrest to call this his "most extreme rock climb." And it certainly was.

Photograph by David Anschicks. Courtesy of David Anschicks.

COLORADO CLIMBERS AND COMPANIES

Betsy Strong Cowles Partridge (1902–1974). For the first 30 years of her life, there was no indication that Betsy Strong would become Colorado's first truly international mountain climber. A Vassar graduate, she moved to Colorado Springs when she married Alfred Cowles. In 1933, her father, John Strong, sensed that the marriage was foundering and invited her to accompany him on a mountain climbing trip to Switzerland. Betsy quickly fell in love with the sport.

In 1941, Cowles and her companions, one of whom was legendary Teton guide Paul Petzoldt, made three first ascents in the Santa Marta Range of northern Colombia. She climbed extensively in Switzerland and in Wyoming's Tetons, making several first ascents and many more as the first female. Betsy also climbed in the Canadian Rockies, New England, and the Wind Rivers of Wyoming. A devoted member of both the American Alpine Club and the Pikes Peak Group of the Colorado Mountain Club, she finished climbing all the then-known Fourteeners in Colorado in 1949.

In 1950, Cowles was the only woman in a party of five to make the first reconnaissance by westerners of the Khumbu region of Nepal. Betsy, who had learned photography from her father, was the official photographer for the party. Organized by Oscar Houston, a New York lawyer, it included his son, Charles Houston, MD, and famed British climber H. W. Tilman. Betsy called it "The Trip of a Lifetime." This was the same approach route later used by the successful British Everest Expedition of 1953.

In 1958, Betsy married a US Air Force four-star general, Earle "Pat" Partridge. Betsy took up flying and Earle took up mountaineering. In 1968, the couple climbed Kilimanjaro in Africa, and in 1970 they made a 25-day trek in western Nepal with Laney and Bill House.

Betsy Cowles. Later Betsy Cowles Partridge, Betsy climbed throughout the West and throughout the world in a long career.

Courtesy of University of Wyoming.

Betsy gave frequent talks and wrote entertaining and detailed articles and journals about her adventures. Music and art were also important parts of her life, and she left behind many stunning black-and-white prints as well as color slides. Charming and gregarious, Betsy Cowles Partridge hobnobbed with prominent men and women all over the world; yet, as she once said, "My best friends are mountain people."

Robert Ormes (1904–1994). The name Ormes is synonymous with Colorado's mountains. Beginning in 1952 with the first edition of his *Guide to the Colorado Mountains*, Bob Ormes wrote descriptions of the routes on the state's summits that were required reading before a trip. Born in Colorado Springs, Bob attended Colorado College and later taught English there. Among his notable climbs were a second ascent of Crestone Needle's Ellingwood Arête, and ascent of Chimney Peak with San Juan Mountaineer Mel Griffiths, and early attempts on Shiprock. Ormes was also a historian and cartographer who tracked abandoned railroad grades, published books identifying mountain skylines, and chronicled the history of all of Colorado's incorporated railroads. But his most-quoted line may be his tongue-in-cheek description of the route on Lizard Head: "When you reach the base, take picture and go home."

Alice Holubar (1907–1968). At first, Alice Freudenberg Holubar resisted getting into the outdoor equipment business. While her husband, Roy, was an instructor in the Engineering Department at the University of Colorado, Alice taught German to graduate students and led weekly "German sings." Then in 1946, after Roy became chair of the CMC's Boulder Group, he purchased a truckload of army surplus sleeping bags to sell to CMC members. A year later, Roy and Alice opened an outdoor equipment business in the basement of their Boulder home. A superb

Success! Joe Stettner and Robert Ormes (right) reflect on their climb of Stettners Ledges, the second known ascent, in 1942.

Courtesy of Colorado Mountain Club Archives.

seamstress, Alice began sewing mountaineering clothes and sleeping bags. For the latter, she designed diamond-wedged baffles, which distributed the down so it didn't collect in the bottom of the bag, added down collars, and used rip-stop nylon. Holubar bags and custom-made clothing quickly became the gold standard for American mountaineers during the 1950s and 1960s. Alice's fluency in German and her family connections in her homeland (well-known mountaineer Karl Blodig was her uncle) gave Holubar's an edge in importing European equipment such as ice axes and leather boots. Although Roy was an avid climber and one of the founders of Rocky Mountain Rescue, Alice was best known for her extraordinary warmth and hospitality, which sometimes extended to feeding her customers.

Colorado Connections to the 1963 American Everest Expedition—
In 1994, when Sir Edmund Hillary was on Pearl Street in Boulder, a woman whose book he was signing mentioned that she'd been to Nepal several times. He replied, "Everyone in Boulder has been to Nepal and half of them have climbed Everest."

Of course that's an exaggeration, but the fact remains that Coloradans have been involved in attempts to summit the world's highest mountain going back to the very first American expedition. That effort took place in 1963, 10 years after the British team of Hillary and Tensing Norgay made the mountain's first ascent.

In the style of the era, the American Expedition included 19 climbers, 32 Sherpas, and 909 porters who carried 27 tons of gear. Al Auten was to be in charge of radio communications. His fellow CMC member, Dick Pownall, was, to quote James Ramsey Ullman, "majordomo of food boxes (which was enough to keep any man occupied)." Auten and Pownall were from Denver.

Alice Holubar at Work. After World War II, the manufacture of mountaineering equipment became a cottage industry. Here Alice Holubar makes some of the innovative and high-quality equipment that the family store in Boulder became known for. The North Face acquired the enterprise in the later 20th century, a time when the development of clothing and equipment became ever more focused on big business.

Photograph by Josephine Robertson. Courtesy of Janet N. and David Robertson.

Hiking into Everest Base Camp. By the end of 2008, there had been 4,102 ascents to the summit by about 2,700 climbers. By the end of 2009, the mountain had claimed the lives of 216 people.

Courtesy of www.everestpeaceproject.org and Tonya Clement.

Another member was Tom Hornbein, MD, originally from St. Louis, Missouri. He'd gotten hooked on mountains during his summers at the Cheley Camp near Estes Park. While earning a geology degree at the University of Colorado in Boulder, he'd climbed extensively and made several first ascents. After leaving the university, Hornbein moved, but he has since returned to Colorado.

A fourth member of the American team was Barry Bishop, from Cincinnati, Ohio. While growing up, he'd spent summers at the

YMCA Camp near Estes Park and been a member of the CMC's Denver Juniors Group, which hiked and climbed all over the state.

The American Everest Expedition purchased tents, parkas, survival suits, seven cable ladders, and several other items from Gerry Mountain Sports. Its innovative owner was CMC member Gerry Cunningham. He lived near Ward, west of Boulder.

On May 22, Bishop and Luke Jerstad became the second and third Americans to summit Everest. (Jim Whittaker and Sherpa Nawang Gombu had preceded them by two weeks.) All climbed by the Southeast Ridge.

A few hours later, Hornbein and Willi Unsoeld stood on top of Everest, having made an epic first ascent via the West Ridge. Eventually all four climbers reconnected as night came on. At 28,000 feet, they huddled together without tents or sleeping bags. Miraculously, they survived, although Bishop and Unsoeld lost toes and fingers. At dawn they resumed their descent, met by David Dingman, MD, who gave up his chance for the summit in order to assist them.

In addition to being the first to climb the West Ridge, Hornbein and Unsoeld were the first to traverse Mount Everest. The 1963 American Expedition had been an extraordinary success.

Layton Kor (1938–). Kor was dubbed "Layton, the great one," renowned as one of the strongest, most determined climbers ever to tie in to the end of a rope. His climbing began when he took his dad's geologist pick to the Manitou sandstone west of Colorado Springs and used it as an ice ax. Next came the rite of passage of many climbers in the 1950s—an inept climb of Boulder's Third Flatiron with hemp rope and army surplus pitons. Kor became a bricklayer to pay his bills, but he lived to climb. He was on the cutting edge of the technical standards

Layton Kor in Glenwood Canyon. Kor was a major figure in the development of big-wall climbing in the mid-20th century.

Courtesy of Colorado Mountain Club Archives.

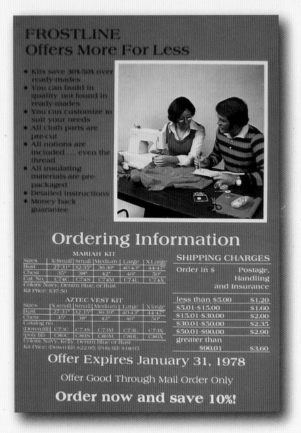

Frostline Ad. This famous business manufactured the tents, sleeping bags, vests, and other equipment that mountaineers sewed together (which meant another skill that climbers needed for a time). But these kits saved financially pressed baby boomers about 50 percent of the cost needed for outdoor equipment.

Courtesy of Dale Johnson.

of the day: the Diagonal on Longs Peak with Ray Northcutt (1959, 5.9 A3); the Yellow Spur on Redgarden Wall in Eldorado Canyon with David Dornan (1960, 5.9 A1); and the Yellow Wall, the second route on the Diamond on Longs Peak, with Charles Roskosz (1962, 5.8 A4). Kor also pioneered such desert classics as the Kor-Ingalls route on Castleton Tower with Huntley Ingalls (1961) and the Mitten Thumb with Steve Komito (1964). Along the way, Kor climbed with the greats of the golden age of big-wall climbing: Royal Robbins, Yvon Chouinard, Chuck Pratt, Steve Roper, and Fred Beckey. As Kor himself wrote in retrospect, "Could I really have been that driven, obsessed, single-minded individual that memory undeniably suggests?" Yes, he was.[5]

Frostline Kits—If you did any skiing or climbing in the late 1960s and early 1970s, odds are that you had some make-it-yourself gear from Frostline. If you were a guy, you enrolled in a home economics course or begged a girlfriend to do the sewing chores. Either way, that still left you carefully searing the edges of nylon squares with a candle and turning countless packets of down inside out with the end of a yardstick. Founded by Dale Johnson of Boulder, Frostline kits were all the rage because they were inexpensive—not counting one's own labor—were of good quality, and fit the self-sufficient free spirit of those years.

Micha Morgan Ascends Blanca Peak Northwest Summit Ridge, November 2010. Winter mountaineering became an ever more important focus of climbers in the later part of the 20th century.

Photograph by Jim Di Napoli. Courtesy of Jim Di Napoli.

Shoshoni Peak. Shoshoni Peak lies in the heart of the Indian Peaks Wilderness Area.

Photograph by Christopher J. Case. Courtesy of Christopher J. Case.

CHAPTER 4

BORROWING FROM OUR CHILDREN

CHRISTOPHER J. CASE

A true conservationist is a man who knows that the world is not given by his fathers, but borrowed from his children.

—John James Audubon

The Colorado experience is defined by remarkable moments: scrambling across a serrated ridgeline as building winds swirl; arching back to digest the full beauty, staggering volume, and ancient poise of a massif in morning light; stumbling upon that rarely seen moose dipping his tongue into the reeds. Many of us expend great energy in pursuit of these humbling moments. But most of us devoted to touching the wild also know that superior fervor is, and was, essential for the eternal protection of these lands.

The Colorado Mountain Club has shown such devotion and worked tirelessly throughout its history to preserve Colorado's wild places. In fact, protecting Colorado's marvelous and varied landscapes—and the indelible experiences that can be had only within them—has been a fundamental ambition of the club since its founding in 1912. The role that members played in the establishment of Rocky Mountain National Park, a mere three years after the club's birth, has been well documented. Of equal importance is its role in the park's designation as a wilderness area in 2009. But there was more to Colorado wildlands than that famed slice of Rocky Mountain terrain.

Endorsing
A Rocky Mountain National Park

Whereas. There is pending in Congress a bill for the establishment of *The Rocky Mountain National Park* in the Front Range of Colorado, including the high peaks of the Estes Park region, Longs Peak and Arapahoe; and

Whereas. There is now no National recreation ground set apart in the characteristic high Rocky Mountain area nor any mountain National Park easily accessible to the residents of the Mississippi Valley and the western and southwestern prairie states; and

Whereas. The area as described in the proposed bill includes many of the typical, striking and best features of the highest area in the Rocky Mountain chain, and particularly Long's Peak (altitude 14,285 feet), Arapahoe Peaks and Arapahoe Glacier (the largest glacier in the Central Rocky Mountains), innumerable lakes and a score of lesser peaks over 12,000 feet in altitude, as well as wide stretches of the great alpine areas above timberline which are so attractive and accessible features of this mountain district, and

Whereas. The park area includes almost exclusively high tracts of alpine and sub-alpine territory, nearly all more than two miles above the level of the sea and without lumbering, agricultural, mining or other possibilities comparable to its value as a scenic, scientific and recreation ground;

Resolved. That *The Colorado Mountain Club* endorses the project for *The Rocky Mountain National Park* and urges upon its members and friends, the western delegations in Congress, the press of America and the United States at large, the advisability of setting-aside this area as a National play-ground before the acquisition of large tracts of privately owned land makes the project more difficult of accomplishment.

The Colorado Mountain Club.

Denver, Colorado, 1914.

Endorsement by the Colorado Mountain Club.
In 1914, the Colorado Mountain Club was in the midst of a campaign to establish a new national park in the Rocky Mountains. This notecard eloquently endorses the club's position on establishing such a "National play-ground."

Courtesy of Colorado Mountain Club Archives.

Colorado Mountain Club

A Lecture By
CHARLES BOWMAN HUTCHINS
Famous Bird Artist, Field Naturalist and Ornithic Singer

"AMERICA'S SEVEN GREATEST SONG-BIRDS"

Tuesday Evening, October 19, 1920, 8 o'clock
AUDITORIUM, WOLCOTT SCHOOL, 1400 MARION ST., DENVER

Mr. Hutchins has delighted and inspired hundreds of thousands to a fuller understanding and greater appreciation of outdoor America, and received pledges from thousands of children that they will help protect their feathered friends, and spread the gospel of their conservation. He is a pastel artist of unusual merit, and during his talk paints colored pictures with great rapidity.

His programs, though instructive, are highly entertaining, the result of long and patient study and actual field experience.

Admission free to Colorado Mountain Club members and their friends. Bring the children.

PROGRAM COMMITTEE,
A. Haanstad, Chairman.

For the Birds. The Colorado Mountain Club hosted innumerable lectures and presentations by some of the most renowned naturalists, artists, and mountain advocates of the time.

Courtesy of Colorado Mountain Club Archives.

Between these two monumental achievements, numerous feats of conservation have sprung from the club. Perhaps these other successes aren't so easily remembered, but they are part of a significant catalog of triumphs that collectively and continuously answered the club's call to preservation, protection, and access.

In 1915, after theft and vandalism plagued paleontologist Earl Douglass's efforts to excavate a quarry in northwestern Colorado, Douglass petitioned for the lands to be protected as a national monument. He was successful. On October 4, 1915, President Woodrow Wilson proclaimed the 80-acre site as Dinosaur National Monument.

In the 1930s, the club set out to learn more about this remote canyon country. First aroused in 1933 by CMC President Garrat B. Van Wagenen, interest steadily grew in exploring the area. Subsequently, efforts increased to protect an area greatly expanded beyond those original 80 acres. More than a half dozen articles about the great canyons of the Green and Yampa rivers appeared in the pages of *Trail & Timberline* between 1934 and 1937, reflecting the numerous trips that were taken to the canyons. In 1934, members Van Wagenen, Edmund B. Rogers, and Robert Niedrach enjoyed a flight over the landscape, with Niedrach making "a number of still and moving pictures." In a few moments of flight, Rogers was able to observe the general topography and scope of a landscape that, a few months before, he had tirelessly studied in detail during a two-week pack trip on behalf of the National Park Service.

"There is something artificial, something almost unnatural about the entrance to Lodore," wrote Rogers, referring to the plunging gateway of Lodore Canyon, a crumbling, upturned canyon cut by the Green River. "Within sight of it, it fascinates and holds one's attention. [John Wesley] Powell records the depressing effect it had on his party. There is something almost sinister about it."[1]

In 1936, under the leadership of Richard Morris, the CMC set out to explore what it was calling "the last frontier of Colorado"—to bring back tangible evidence of the existence of archaeological remains, confirm the romantic stories of the area's early history, and capture a photographic impression of the beauty of the region. A survey of the frontier—named the Canyon of Lodore–Yampa River Reconnaissance of 1936—was born, and revealed the club's enthusiasm for pioneering

Lodore. The 1930s saw more than a half dozen articles, trip reports, and endorsements for the expansion of Dinosaur National Monument. The famed explorer John Wesley Powell explored the Gates of Lodore, which rise from the banks of the Green River, on his exploration of the West, including the Grand Canyon, in 1869. "There is something almost sinister about it," wrote Edmund Rogers about the Gates of Lodore, located in Colorado's Dinosaur National Monument, which he explored in the 1930s.

Photograph by Airphoto/Jim Wark. Courtesy of Airphoto/Jim Wark.

exploration: "Two thousand-foot vertical canyon walls . . . a wild, raging river hemmed in by solid rock . . . a river doubling back within 200 feet of itself . . . pictographs . . . pre-historic cliff dwellings . . . the home of notorious bad men . . . unexplored . . . unmapped . . . uninhabited . . . the last frontier of Colorado."[2]

The effort that members put toward exploring, surveying, and promoting such special country amounted to a grand endorsement for its protection. In 1938, President Franklin D. Roosevelt expanded Dinosaur National Monument to 204,000 acres, which included the scenic canyons of the Green and Yampa rivers.

Ironically, after a lull in the club's efforts, it was an issue facing Dinosaur that brought conservation back to the forefront of its attention. "There was no compelling conservation issue until 1954," recalled Janet N. Robertson, a longtime member of the club and conservation devotee. That year, the Bureau of Reclamation proposed the construction of two dams within the heart of the monment— one at Split Mountain and one at Echo Park, where the Green and Yampa rivers join. "And then," Robertson said, "the Colorado Mountain Club blew it."[3]

Though the majority of members who were surveyed opposed the construction of the dams, the CMC Board of Directors chose not to take a stand. Fortunately, the Colorado Springs and Boulder groups of the club circumvented the state board's decision and, alongside The Wilderness Society and the Sierra Club, were able to prevent the dams from being built.

Beyond the controversy that arose within the CMC, the conservation victory was bittersweet: Congress still passed the Colorado River Storage Act in March 1956, which authorized several other large dams: Glen Canyon (which formed Lake Powell), Flaming Gorge, Navajo, and the Curecanti unit dams on the Gunnison River. Nevertheless, the publicity surrounding the dams of Dinosaur resulted in a national concern that no public lands were safe from development. This perfect storm of media attention, social awareness, and the shifting of powers created the atmosphere that allowed conservation organizations to pursue a system of wilderness preservation, which they had sought for decades.

The movement toward a national wilderness system originated in the first half of the 20th century. As early as 1925, Aldo Leopold had promoted a vision for a "definite national policy," advocating for a system of wilderness areas involving both national parks and forests. In 1934, Bob Marshall built upon this idea with his endorsement of a "nationwide wilderness plan," suggesting the need to protect, by statutory law, the parks and forests and to extend protection to the public lands administered by what became the Bureau of Land Management, Indian reservations, and state and private lands.

In 1945, Howard Zahniser emerged at the head of the wilderness movement when he was appointed executive secretary of The Wilderness Society and editor of the organization's publication, *Living Wilderness*. Zahniser used the magazine to educate a wider public on the advantages of wilderness preservation and to alert supporters to emerging threats to surviving wildlands. In the early 1950s, he led the pivotal campaign to preserve Echo Park and prevent the construction of the proposed dam within Dinosaur National Monument. This celebrated conservation victory brought the wilderness movement intense publicity and garnered the political clout to push for federal wilderness legislation.

On the local scale, numerous organizations and groups like the Colorado Mountain Club began to engage on the issue. On November 14, 1958, E. H. Brunquist, a representative of the club's board of directors and conservation committee, attended a hearing in Albuquerque, New Mexico, in support of a bill to establish the National Wilderness Preservation System. Hotly debated, the proposed bill was receiving considerable criticism despite numerous revisions and concessions. Ironically, those opposed to the bill struggled with many of the same perceived problems that wilderness opponents grapple with today: They contended the bill would "strike a blow at the very heart of the state's economy and the ability of its people to make a decent living"; they were under the impression that "the wilderness areas [could] be used for recreation and not much else"; and they were afraid that designation would "lock the treasure chest of the U.S. and throw away the key." For the next six years, debate persisted over the language and goals of the proposed bill; Brunquist continued to represent the club's interest for a national system for wilderness protection.

In 1961, the club's conservation work was further invigorated when Dick Guadagno became director of the conservation committee. Soon after, a college student, Roger Fuehrer, led the club into the age of environmentalism.

For many reasons—politics, polemics, and principles, not to mention the illuminating tale of Rachel Carson's *Silent Spring*—the

Snow Peak. The mountain stands near Deluge Lake in the Eagles Nest Wilderness Area.

Photograph by Christopher J. Case. Courtesy of Christopher J. Case.

Overlooking 10th Mountain Hut. Though pictured here in summer, this shelter was one of nearly 40 huts built for cross-country skiers in honor of the men and women of the 10th Mountain Division, which trained at Camp Hale in the Central Rockies during Word War II.

Reduction woodblock print by Leon Loughridge. Courtesy of Leon Loughridge.

1960s saw a national surge in concern for conservation, mirrored within the CMC.

Undeniably, the initial effort was small. After the CMC Board of Directors refused Fuehrer's request for $100 in funding, a sympathetic board member secretly gave him money to ride the train to San Francisco and attend the Sierra Club's biennial Wilderness Convention of 1961. The convention proved to be a crushing blow, but an inspiring one. Fuehrer was largely ignored by environmentalists who felt powerless against Colorado anti-environmentalist and pro-dam US Representative Wayne Aspinall. The Colorado congressman served as chairman of the House Committee on Interior and Insular Affairs, and he was openly doing his best to prevent the bill from being discussed and voted upon on the House floor. *Harper's* magazine declared a showdown: Wayne Aspinall versus the People of the United States.

David Brower, the first executive director of the Sierra Club, said that the environmental movement in the 1950s and 1960s had seen "dream after dream dashed on the stony countenance of Wayne Aspinall." Fuehrer returned, however, determined to achieve one goal from within the club: Find an issue, form a committee, and wrap it in a philosophy that confirmed their principles.

The conservation committee that formed—including mountaineer and author Hugh Kingery; future Colorado Governor Dick Lamm; Aldo Leopold's daughter, Estella; Eleanor Roosevelt's niece, Amy; and six others—started and succeeded with a local issue: banning billboards. Then they quickly moved on to that national issue that had so captivated the nation: creation of the National Wilderness Preservation System. The committee spurred a concerted, determined, and fruitful commitment to the salvation of wilderness lands in Colorado. As a result, the influence of the CMC within the wilderness movement was recognized statewide. In January 1962, a leaflet was prepared by the Wilderness Committee of Colorado and sent to the club's Denver Group members. They were encouraged to join the organization in support of the wilderness bill. Brunquist, meanwhile, urged the members of the club to lend their support to the cause. "'Grass roots' support might well tip the scales in favor of passage of an effective bill," he wrote. Multiple *Trail & Timberline* articles appeared that year highlighting the importance of supporting a federal system designed to protect wildlands throughout the nation.

During 1964, the conservation committee focused its attention on the debate in Washington over the proposed wilderness bill. Working from an apartment that Fuehrer shared with three other CMC members, the young group was able to persuade countless people to testify at the Denver hearings on behalf of the bill. As Fuehrer wrote, so many people testified that Congress in Washington actually adjourned for two days while the congressmen in Denver heard three days of testimony—two days longer than originally scheduled.

After decades of grueling deliberation and debate, and through the efforts of organizations large and small, the wilderness movement was finally on the cusp of a great triumph. Howard Zahniser imbued the final bill with his characteristic eloquence and philosophy:

> *A wilderness, in contrast with those areas where man and his own works dominate the landscape, is hereby recognized as an area where the earth and its community of life are untrammeled by man, where man himself is a visitor who does not remain.*

The Maroon Bells. The famous Maroon Bells stand at the center of the Maroon Bells–Snowmass Wilderness Area, one of five original wilderness areas created in Colorado in 1964 by the Wilderness Act.

Painting by William Durham.
Courtesy of Kirkland Museum of Fine & Decorative Art, Denver.

Sheep near Crater Lake. The Wilderness Act does not preclude the possibility of grazing in wilderness areas, but in some areas, scenes like this one, depicting sheep near Crater Lake in 1952, have become increasingly rare.

Photograph by Norman Neuhoff. Courtesy of Janet N. Robertson.

On September 3, 1964, the Wilderness Act was signed into law, creating the National Wilderness Preservation System and requiring an act of Congress to designate any further wilderness area.

Sadly, Zahniser never tasted the fruit of his devotion. He passed away less than six months before the act was signed. But the impact of his dedication lives on. Through his commitment to the cause, the wilderness movement succeeded in creating a federal system of preservation that protects wildlands in perpetuity.

In Colorado, the Wilderness Act of 1964 ensured lasting protection for five tracts of rich landscape: La Garita, Maroon Bells–Snowmass, Mount Zirkel, Rawah, and West Elk wilderness areas. This original class—now constituting 720,553 acres of protected land—was but a small portion of the 9.1 million acres of wilderness designated throughout the United States that year.

Successes continued in the age of environmentalism. Later that decade, under the direction of Estella Leopold and Beatrice Willard, the club's fervent conservation ethic led it to spearhead the protection of what many were realizing was "one of the world's outstanding natural museums of prehistoric plant and animal life." In August 1966, an article appeared in *Trail & Timberline* that detailed the great fossils and petrified remains of the Florissant lake shales west of Colorado Springs and called for members to contact their congressmen to support the establishment of Florissant Fossil Beds National Monument.

When housing developments began to spring up within the proposed protected area, a CMC trip was organized to detail the encroachment. Subsequent studies by the trip participants led to reports being sent to the National Park Service with recommendations for boundary changes.

Leopold and Willard led the cause to protect the land—and its wealth of paleontological discoveries—by forming a group they called Defenders of Florissant. Supported by the innovative tactics of the group's lawyers, who secured an injunction, this sliver of land, shaped by volcanic eruptions some 34 million years ago, was saved from being subdivided into thousands of homes. On August 20, 1969, the area gained protection as Florissant Fossil Beds National Monument.

But the field of conservation was soon to change. Not only were environmental causes gaining national attention and stirring national passions, but also the cause for environmental action was becoming highly complex. The passage of the National Environmental Policy Act (NEPA) on January 1, 1970, created a requirement that environmental policy be considered through federal agency decision making and that the public be given the chance to review environmental assessments and impact statements. Essentially, protecting the environment became even more of a game for experts—and those who could handle mounds of paperwork.

Crusaders, 1994. Estella Leopold (left), Beatrice Willard, and Vim Wright helped protect the exquisite paleontological sites of the Florissant Fossil Beds National Monument.

Photograph by Dorothy H. Bradley.
Courtesy of Florissant Fossil Beds National Monument.

FLORISSANT FOSSIL BEDS NATIONAL MONUMENT

The struggle to create Florissant Fossil Beds National Monument reflects the battles incurred in creating many national parks and wilderness areas. It began in the 1960s, when Dr. Beatrice (Bettie) Willard, Dr. Estella Leopold, and, later, Vim Wright teamed up in a fight to save one of Colorado's most remarkable places, the Florissant Fossil Beds, one of the most important deposits of plant and insect fossils in the world.

Bettie Willard, a Californian born in 1925, was the daughter of an artist/photographer who had studios in Palm Springs (winter) and Mammoth Lakes (summer), both towns in California. Encouraged to be independent, Willard spent her childhood exploring, often by herself, and learning the names of the wildflowers.

During World War II, a retired entomology professor from the University of Colorado, Dr. Theodore Cockerell, became curator of the local museum in Palm Springs. From him, Willard first heard of the world-famous fossil beds near Florissant, Colorado.

Although she encountered prejudice against female biologists unless they were high school teachers, Willard persisted. Eventually, in 1963, she earned a PhD in ecology from the University of Colorado. Her research on the impacts of humans on the tundra in Rocky Mountain National Park has had a huge influence on national park policy throughout the United States and elsewhere.

After a stint teaching in Oregon, she moved back to Boulder, where she worked for the Thorne Ecological Institute from 1965 to 1972, serving as its president for the last two years. And she renewed her friendship with Estella Leopold, whom she'd met at the University of California, Berkeley.

Born in 1917 in Madison, Wisconsin, Leopold was the daughter of one of America's most famous biologists, Aldo Leopold. (His collection of environmental essays, *Sand County Almanac*, published in 1949, has become a classic.) After earning her doctorate in plant sciences from Yale University in 1956, Estella moved to Denver to work for the US Geological Survey's biological laboratory.

Willard and Leopold were appalled that one of the richest and most diverse deposits of plant and insect fossils in the world, near Florissant, was under assault. Privately owned, it was threatened by a huge housing development. Fossil hunters were rampant. At the time Leopold was chair of the Colorado Mountain Club's conservation committee, while Willard was an energetic member of the Sierra Club; she later joined the CMC. (Leopold credits Hugh Kingery for getting her started in conservation.) The two women put their considerable energy and expertise into protecting 6,000 acres of the threatened fossil beds.

The resulting publicity attracted the notice of V. Crane "Vim" Wright, an environmental activist living in Denver. She was involved in founding the Audubon Society in Denver and hosted the notorious Oil Shale Breakfast Club.

Born in Istanbul in 1926 and adopted by an American military family who nurtured her love of nature, Vim Wright was raised in Baltimore. After reading about the threats to the fossil beds, she phoned Estella Leopold and offered to help any way she could, which included throwing herself in front of a bulldozer. She later repeated the offer on a radio

A petrified tree stump.

Photograph by Lindsay J. Walker. Courtesy of Florissant Fossil Beds National Monument.

show, but never had to carry it out. At the time of the controversy, Wright was head of the Colorado Open Space Coordinating Council, an influential grassroots organization. However, during the Florissant fight, she was careful to separate her official position from her personal passion.

The triumvirate stirred up public sympathy for their cause, aided by lawyer Vic Yannacone. Finally, in 1969, President Richard Nixon signed legislation that created Florissant Fossil Beds National Monument. The Colorado Wildlife Federation named Bettie Willard and Estella Leopold "Conservationists of the Year."

Willard went on to become a member of the President's Council on Environmental Quality, appointed by Nixon. She made many trips to Alaska and provided substantial input about how to mitigate the impacts of the Alaska Pipeline, which was then being built, on migrating caribou.

After moving back to Boulder, she taught classes and wrote several books, the best known of which is *The Land Above the Trees*, with co-author Ann Zwinger. In the late 1970s, Willard took on her most difficult role, that of creating the Department of Environmental Sciences and Engineering Ecology at Colorado School of Mines. She died in 2003.

Leopold, too, had a distinguished career. After working at the US Geological Survey for 20 years, she moved on to work for the University of Washington. There she served as director of the Quaternary Research Center, as a professor of botany and forest resources, and, later, as a professor of botany and environmental studies. She is an adjunct professor emeritus and lives in Seattle.

In 1977, Wright moved to Washington, where she founded many environmental organizations and served as assistant director of the Institute for Environmental Studies until the University of Washington closed the department. Vim Wright died in 2003, three days shy of her 77th birthday.

Colorado's Mountain Desert. The Sangre de Cristo Mountains loom over Great Sand Dunes National Park, much of which became a wilderness area in 1976.

Photograph by Dave Cooper. Courtesy of Dave Cooper.

Coupled with powerful new laws like the Wilderness Act and the Wild and Scenic Rivers Act of 1968, the NEPA policies created a challenge: how to most effectively put these new conservation tools to use. There was enormous potential for protection, but the novel legislative process created a steep learning curve.

Beginning in 1970, the CMC involved itself in a number of wilderness proposals. On July 1, the first wilderness hearing for one of Colorado's national monuments was held in Alamosa. The intent was to discuss the designation of Great Sand Dunes National Monument as wilderness. A major controversy involved the eastern boundary, where a local concessionaire planned to rent dune buggies.

Also during the summer of 1970, the CMC participated in hearings for the Weminuche, Uncompahgre, and Mount Sneffels wilderness areas. The proposed Weminuche faced particularly vehement opposition from loggers, miners, and officials in Hinsdale County who were promoting a highway project between Lake City and Pagosa Springs. More than twice the size of the largest wilderness area in the state, the Weminuche could almost as easily never have been designated without the support generated by the CMC's conservation committee. Yet, over the course of the next decade, protection ultimately prevailed with the creation of Weminuche, Uncompahgre, Mount Sneffels, and Great Sand Dunes wilderness areas.

At the same time, Colorado was facing its greatest wilderness controversy in the battle over the Eagles Nest Wilderness Area. In September 1970, the club began advocating for the preservation of this powerful and plentiful landscape. "The wild Gore Range is untrammeled and wonderfully wild," wrote Hugh Kingery, editor of *Trail & Timberline* at the time. "Only a handful of its peaks bear names—adding to the wild aura. Many of these summits have never felt the climber's foot. We urge you to write your support to the Forest Service."

Colorful Colorado. Autumn turns the Deluge Lake Trail in the Eagles Nest Wilderness Area into a corridor of color. In 1976, after much effort and many negotiations, preservationists saved the area from development.

Photograph by Christopher J. Case. Courtesy of Christopher J. Case.

Unfortunately, the same plentiful natural resources that made Eagles Nest so precious to conservationists were coveted by numerous public and private industries. As Mark Pearson wrote in his *Complete Guide to Colorado's Wilderness Areas*, "a formidable array of powerful interests lined up against the Eagles Nest Wilderness legislation in 1976: the US Department of Transportation, Kaibab Industries (a major timber company), and the Denver Water Department." All wanted something from the land, whether water, wood, or a highway corridor. Ultimately, a series of compromises prevented the area from being eviscerated. In 1976, it became a 133,000-plus–acre wilderness.

Only two years later, controversy raged over another jaggedly attractive, but heavily used, region—the popular Indian Peaks area. The CMC became one of a number of organizations supporting the creation of the wilderness area there. At a hearing in support of the bill in July 1978, the protection of the area's "great aesthetic, biological, and spiritual value" was promoted as "another step toward the restoration of an ancient balance of knowledge, heart, and spirit, nourished by the earth and guarded by the wise."

Clearly, the serrated ridges and rough-hewn summits of the Indian Peaks were visually stunning, its glaciers were thought to be the southernmost permanently found in North America, and its lakes and drainages offered an abundance of precious water. Disputes erupted, however, over whether an area that saw so much visitation should become wilderness, or whether the Indian Peaks could in fact meet the requirements for solitude demanded by the Wilderness Act.

In October 1978 it was decided that through careful management, the required opportunities for solitude could indeed be found within the Indian Peaks wilderness and that the impacts of extensive recreational use could be mitigated by limiting access to the area east of the Continental Divide. More than 75,000 acres were thereby set aside for protection in perpetuity.

Two years later, following on the heels of the Forest Service's Roadless Area Review and Evaluation II (RARE II), the club further strengthened its position on wilderness designation with the creation of a wilderness subcommittee. The state board urged the new committee to "preserve as much quality wilderness as possible."

Still at the helm of the conservation committee, Fuehrer reported that since RARE II was conducted, "club members have shown their deep concern for Colorado's wildlands by contributing money for a special wilderness fund, by participating in the work of the committee, and by writing hundreds of letters at critical times." For months, committee volunteers had contributed thousands of hours of work—writing reports, attending conferences and workshops, lobbying across the state and in Washington, D.C., going on numerous wilderness field studies—toward the passage of a Colorado wilderness bill.

On December 22, 1980, their dedication was rewarded. On that day, no fewer than 14 new wilderness areas were created in the state, including Neota, Never Summer, Raggeds, Lizard Head, Lost Creek, Mount Evans, Mount Massive, Mount Sneffels, Cache La Poudre, Collegiate Peaks, Comanche Peak, Holy Cross, South San

Mount Toll. In 1978, Mount Toll and more than 75,000 acres of the jagged peaks above Boulder became part of the Indian Peaks Wilderness Area.

Photograph by Christopher J. Case. Courtesy of Christopher J. Case.

House Cleaning. Colorado Mountain Club volunteers, under the direction of Roger Fuehrer, were instrumental in the club's conservation ethic in the 1960s, even cleaning cans from a litter-strewn alpine lake.

Photograph by Roger Fuehrer. Courtesy of Roger Fuehrer.

Winter's Rewards. Mount Evans winter's rewards are plenty. The wind-carved snows in the Mount Evans Wilderness Area make for abstract scenery.

Photograph by Christopher J. Case. Courtesy of Christopher J. Case.

Mountains of Reports. Anne Vickery, the club's first conservation staff member, is surrounded by the tools of her trade: reports and more reports.

Photograph by Janet N. Robertson. Courtesy of Janet N. Robertson.

Juan, and Uncompahgre. Under the bill, a number of other existing areas gained considerable additions. These areas now amount to a total of 1,006,871 acres.

In the early 1980s, the CMC's position within the greater wilderness movement underwent significant change. The club hired its first conservation staff member, Anne Vickery, thereby gaining an effective leader for wilderness negotiations. Although support for and involvement in the wilderness movement among the membership varied from area to area, the board of directors ultimately approved the club's stance for more wilderness protection.

In 1993, the Buffalo Peaks, Byers Peak, Fossil Ridge, Greenhorn Mountain, Powderhorn, Ptarmigan Peak, Sangre de Cristo, Sarvis Creek, and Vazquez Peak wilderness areas were designated. Today, they total 469,314 acres of pristine Colorado landscape.

As with most environmental causes today, an individual voice is only as loud as the chorus of which it is a part. Banding together, individuals, organizations, citizens' groups, and conservation coalitions tackle the pursuit of wilderness protection. It may take Congress to enact wilderness law, but each wilderness designation seen in Colorado, as in every state, has started with the inspired, determined, and cooperative advocacy of individuals.

In this way, on March 30, 2009, decades of effort by the club and myriad partners resulted in wilderness designation for more than 2 million acres of wildlands throughout the nation, including the backcountry of Colorado's Rocky Mountain National Park and the Dominguez Canyon Wilderness Area.

The list of the many other accomplishments that have arisen from the club's devotion to "the preservation of forests, flowers, fauna, and natural scenery" is a long one. The historical menu includes a

Under the Rainbow. Little Bear Peak, Ellingwood Point, Blanca Peak, and Mount Lindsey
are bathed in rainbow light in the Sangre de Cristo Wilderness Area.

Photograph by Christopher J. Case. Courtesy of Christopher J. Case.

The Good Woodsman. These signs, created in the early decades of the Colorado Mountain Club, were a product of the CMC's nature protection committee, whose popular campaigns included the creation of literature extolling the virtues of treating nature gently—a new approach at that time.

Courtesy of Colorado Mountain Club Archives.

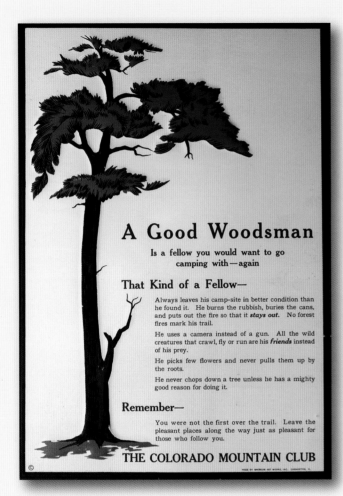

A Good Woodsman

Is a fellow you would want to go camping with—again

That Kind of a Fellow—

Always leaves his camp-site in better condition than he found it. He burns the rubbish, buries the cans, and puts out the fire so that it *stays out.* No forest fires mark his trail.

He uses a camera instead of a gun. All the wild creatures that crawl, fly or run are his *friends* instead of his prey.

He picks few flowers and never pulls them up by the roots.

He never chops down a tree unless he has a mighty good reason for doing it.

Remember—

You were not the first over the trail. Leave the pleasant places along the way just as pleasant for those who follow you.

THE COLORADO MOUNTAIN CLUB

On the Trail—Quandary Peak. Hiking the Fourteeners—the peaks over 14,000 feet high—has become an extremely popular activity for many Coloradans and those from other states and countries. The Colorado Fourteeners Initiative estimates that each year between 500,000 and 750,000 people hike on Colorado's 54 official peaks over 14,000 feet.

Photograph by Anya Byers. Courtesy of Anya Byers.

multitude of wilderness designations; land-use protection; access negotiations; conservation and recreation balancing acts; and smaller, but collectively no less significant, feats. When considering the club's particular successes in protecting Rocky Mountain National Park and Dinosaur and Florissant Fossil Beds national monuments, it becomes clear that the CMC's conservation visionaries were wise enough to know that the world is borrowed from our children.

Colorado will never again see the likes of a grand landscape like that of Rocky Mountain National Park protected in perpetuity. Large, unfragmented landscapes no longer exist, and, furthermore, conservation is a highly regulated beast. Still, the passion to preserve Colorado's remaining wildlands remains.[4]

For the Trail. A work party with Volunteers of Colorado heads into the Indian Peaks Wilderness Area to perform trail maintenance, a staple of environmental work in an age when outdoor recreation has become ever more popular.

Photograph by Janet N. Robertson. Courtesy of Janet N. Robertson.

Gudy Gaskill. Gudy was the leading figure in creating the Colorado Trail, which runs almost 500 miles between Denver and Durango.

Photograph by Christopher J. Case. Courtesy of Christopher J. Case.

CHANGES TO THE LANDSCAPE

As conservation and preservation became key themes in the environmental movement, so, too, did a growing awareness of climate change. By the early 21st century, environmental changes in the Rocky Mountains had become obvious. Recent winters—both in Rocky Mountain National Park and in other parts of Colorado—have not reached temperatures as low as they had in former times. The snow cover isn't as deep, it begins accumulating later and begins melting sooner than it did even several decades ago, and summers have become warmer and dryer. Climate change is altering the environment and the ecology.

Beetle-Infested Trees. These trees, dead and dying on a hillside in Laskey Gulch near Silverthorne, reflect the powerful ecological changes transforming the Rocky Mountains in the early 21st century.

Photograph by Christopher J. Case.
Courtesy of Christopher J. Case.

PINE BEETLES. Pine beetles have seemingly gone on a rampage. Though long a part of Colorado's forests, they thrive in the new environment because the milder winters do not kill as many of the insects as they once did, and the longer, warmer summers make the trees more susceptible to attack. And, according to Dr. Jeffry Mitton of the University of Colorado's Department of Ecology and Evolutionary Biology, the beetles have begun flying two months earlier and attacking trees 2,000 feet higher in elevation than they once did—attacks that extend to the state's magnificent limber pines known to live for well over 1,000 years. The result is the death of forests of pine trees.

Limber Pines. Formerly healthy limber pines like these near Rainbow Curve in Rocky Mountain National Park became the victims in the growing scourge of pine beetles at ever higher altitudes.

Photograph by Jeffry Mitton. Courtesy of Jeffry Mitton.

GLACIAL RETREAT. Another impact of climate change in Colorado is the retreat of ancient glaciers along the Front Range and elsewhere in the state. Many examples of this trend may be found, but Rowe Glacier in Rocky Mountain National Park in particular demonstrates what is happening to cirque glaciers (those in bowl-like depressions on mountainsides), along with "permanent" snowfields in the park, the Indian Peaks to the south, and elsewhere.

The documented history of this glacier goes back to 1881 when Israel Rowe, a hunter, discovered what he called "the biggest snowfield in the Rockies" north of Hagues Peak. He came upon it while looking for bears that were attracted to the high country by the smell of decaying grasshoppers embedded in snowbanks. They had fallen out of the sky while swarming from Utah.

Word about the huge snowfield spread. In 1884, William Hallett, a recent graduate of the Massachusetts Institute of Technology, explored it by himself. After he fell into a "fissure two feet wide and 30 feet deep, its bottom filled with icy water," from which he barely managed to escape, he became convinced that he'd fallen into a crevasse. A few years later, Dr. G. M. Stone, a geology professor at Colorado College in Colorado Springs, confirmed that Rowe's discovery was, indeed, not a snowfield, but a true glacier. It came to be named for Hallett, but in 1932, the US Board on Geographic Names changed the name to Rowe Glacier.

Two photographs of Rowe Glacier clearly indicate the impact of climate change in the more than 125 years since its discovery. Circa 1888, Bostonian mountain climber Frederick Chapin visited the glacier and photographed it. A year later, he published the pictures in his book, *Mountaineering in Colorado*. Then in 2010, two Colorado Mountain Club photographers captured the glacier again. The two sets of photographs taken at the beginning and end of this long era dramatically depict the impact of climate change on Rowe Glacier and, by extension, glaciers throughout the region.[5]

Rowe Glacier, August 2, 1888.

Photography by Frederick Chapin. Courtesy of Rocky Mountain National Park Archives.

Rowe Glacier, August 8, 2010.

Photograph by Glenn G. and Margie Patterson. Courtesy of Glenn G. and Margie Patterson.

WILDFIRES. Although fire has been a fact of life in Colorado for its entire history, the first decade of the 21st century witnessed a series of especially destructive fires. In June 2002, the Hayman Fire near the Tarryall River destroyed 138,000 acres and 133 homes. In September 2010, the Fourmile Canyon Fire west of Boulder burned 6,200 acres and 169 structures, for which $217 million worth of insurance claims were filed. Both fires were caused by human hand, but they and others reflect the growing menace of climate change in the past century and more.

DUSTY SNOW. The phenomenon of dusty snow causes the snow to melt much earlier than it would if this type of snow weren't present. Reporter R. Scott Rappold of Colorado Springs wrote in April 2010 that "for the second year in a row, heavy winds out of the south and west have coated the mountains—the source of Colorado Springs' water—with a layer of reddish-brown dust from the deserts of Utah, Arizona, and New Mexico. The dust absorbs heat from sunlight and melts the snow more quickly."

The western slope has also sustained problems from this cause. The Southern Utah Wilderness Alliance (SUWA) reports that increasingly, research indicates that windborne dust from disturbed desert soil is a factor in the Colorado River's early snowmelt, which reduces flow in the river by 5 percent. And, citing a 2010 article based on research funded by the National Aeronautics and Space Administration (NASA), SUWA notes that the desert soil is disturbed by "grazing, drought, fire, plowing, or vehicles."[6]

CLIMATE CHANGE AND THE ROCKY MOUNTAINS. Global warming is a controversial public issue. Most people believe it exists. A minority deny it. Most people believe it is caused or largely caused by people and industrial development in all its forms. Others deny it. But the scientific studies, the photographic record, and simple observation suggest powerfully that over the two centuries of industrialization, significant and accelerating changes have come to the environment and ecology of the Rocky Mountains.

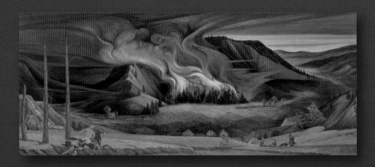

Forest Fire. Born in Kansas, Frank Mechau grew up in Glenwood Springs. He studied art in Denver, Chicago, and Europe, where he became powerfully influenced by cubism, and later taught at the Broadmoor Art Academy in Colorado Springs. This work captures the natural impact of fire in remaking and revitalizing the high country.
Painting by Frank Mechau. Courtesy of Paula Mechau-Michael Mechau Administrator.

Dusty Snow—Ice Lake Basin. Dust on snow accelerates melting and enhances evaporation, promoting drought.
Photograph by Janet N. Robertson. Courtesy of Janet N. Robertson.

Columbine appear along the trail to Arapaho Pass in the Indian Peaks Wilderness Area. The state flower graces innumerable woods and meadows in the high country.

Photograph by Glenn Randall. Courtesy of Glenn Randall.

Sun, Snow, and Solitude. The blue sky and white snow characteristic of Colorado's high country proclaim a marvelous day of cross-country skiing above timberline.

Photograph by Spencer Swanger. Courtesy of Karen B. Morris.

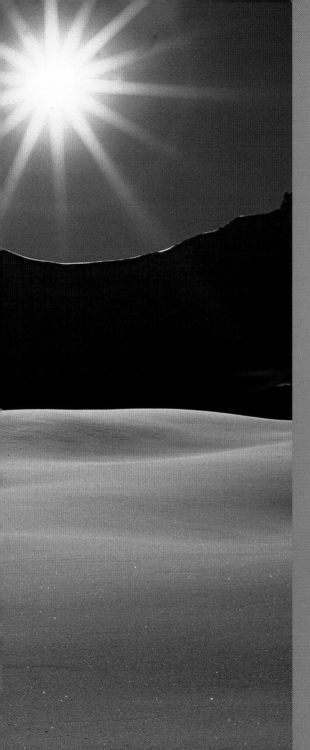

CHAPTER 5

CARVING THE SNOW

JAMES E. FELL, JR.

The grade was still 8% and we knew we had a clear track so we just set sail and went.... Occasionally, we had to brake with our poles for the wind seemed stronger and we felt as if we were flying as the big pine trees sped by.... Around another bend we could see three long switchbacks thru the open timber and tiny Tolland far below. We left the track and went straight down the hill, making big curves, with the perfect powdered snow swirling in the air.... No need to fall—the world was ours.

—MARJORIE PERRY

In the early 1880s, on a warm winter day under a bright and blue sky, Andy Bray edged up the steep slopes of Slot Cut outside of Gunnison, his skis and balance pole slung over his shoulder. Off in the distance he could see the dark shape of a South Park train snaking through the white landscape. He strapped on his skis, checked his equipment, and waited as the train approached. As it chugged into the cut, he pushed off with his pole, charged down the hill, leaped over the cars, and landed safely on the other side. It was another successful train jump, a feat that had made Bray something of a legend in these parts of Colorado.[1]

Colorado Ski Country USA, 1960. As a highly regarded cartographer for the US Geological Survey and collaborator with the Jeppeson Map Company, Hal Shelton applied his techniques in natural-color mapping to art. For his most famous panorama, "Colorado: Ski Country USA," he received a lifetime ski pass to all resorts in Colorado. Shelton put the pass to good use for many decades, He died in Golden in 2004.

Poster by Hal Sheldon. Courtesy of the collection of Wes Brown.

Few skiers engaged in train jumping like Andy Bray, but by the 1880s, skis and skiing were nothing new in Colorado. They came with the gold rush, and they were for work, not play. As early as 1859, miners deep in the mountains used them for travel. In that day, they were called "Norwegian snowshoes" because immigrants from Scandinavia had brought this technique of travel to the United States. The "snowshoes" were long, thick boards curved at the tip, often made from barrel staves, and attached to boots with thick leather straps. Travelers who used them did not have a pole in each hand to help them turn and stay upright the way modern skiers do. Instead, they had a single long balance pole, like the popular high-wire walkers of the day. Norwegian snowshoes resembled modern skis in only a general way.

As the gold rush propelled Colorado's development, skis came into use largely for transportation through the deep snows in the mountains in a time when there were no railroads and only difficult wagon roads. The postal service engaged carriers on skis to move the mail from mining camp to mining camp. Miners, merchants, and various travelers used them to make their way from town to town. Itinerant preachers used them as well, to spread the gospel. The most famous was the Reverend John Dyer, a letter carrier who became known in Colorado history and legend as "the snowshoe itinerant" for his work in carrying the gospel over Hoosier and Boreas passes near Breckenridge on behalf of the Blue River Mission. Skis in essence provided a link between isolated towns, ranches, and mines and the outside world.

At least one mineral rush took place on Norwegian snowshoes. In the winter of 1878/1879, when word reached Leadville of rich silver deposits in the Ten Mile north across Fremont Pass, hundreds departed Leadville on skis. Prospectors, miners, and merchants poured across Fremont Pass in "the fever heat of excitement" for silver. Skis also carried many to Carbonateville, Robinson, Kokomo, and Recen, where they pitched tents in the cold, cut down trees to make log cabins, and dug through deep snow to make claims. "The lack of indications," wrote journalist Frank Fossett, was overcome "by a superabundance of faith." The spring thaw revealed tree stumps six feet high.

Norwegian snowshoes had still other uses. Ranchers used them to gather stray cattle. A midwife at Steamboat Springs had skiers pull her toboggan to patients about to deliver. One newspaper editor reported that at Crested Butte and Irwin, "every man, woman, and child had to learn to ski . . . we had to learn if we wanted to go anywhere." And at the end of the 19th century, residents of Hunters Pass (now Independence Pass), near Aspen, even dismantled homes to make skis to escape starvation. Susan Anderson, the famed "Doc Susie" of Middle Park, skied to see patients. "I've skied into ditches," she wrote, "I've lost my way, now and then, in a blizzard, nothing to get worried about."[2]

Utilitarian purposes aside, by the 1880s skiing was also evolving into a sport. Downhill racing—along with train jumping—emerged in the Gunnison country and elsewhere, and by the end of the century, tourists in Colorado had begun to use skis to enjoy the travel, the views, and the outdoors. "Coasting on snowshoes has taken the place

Pausing on the Slopes. These early skiers display changing technology—ski poles overtaking the older balance pole. The surging popularity of downhill skiing created equally dramatic advances in clothing, ski equipment, and lift technology.

Courtesy of Denver Public Library.

PIONEERS IN SKIING

Carl Howelsen [Karl Hovelsen] (1877–1955). Carl Howelsen's time in Colorado was brief, but his contribution to Colorado skiing was longstanding. Born in Kristiania (now Oslo), Norway, in 1877, and a stonemason and bricklayer by trade, Howelsen emerged as an international ski champion in Europe in both cross-country and jumping events. Escaping hard times there, he came to the United States in 1905. Four years later, he gravitated to Colorado, where he introduced recreational skiing to Denver. After a sojourn in Hot Sulphur Springs, a major hub of skiing in that day, he eventually went on to Steamboat Springs, where he established ski jumping as a national sport. After about a decade in Colorado, he returned to Norway in 1922, where he died in 1955. Howelsen Hill at Steamboat Springs is named in his honor.

of dancing parties ... and "uite a number of our ladies are becoming adept at the art," wrote one resident of Grand County in 1883. Ski racing became popular from Denver across the mountains to the distant, remote San Juans. One Silverton racer was reported to look like "a war horse thirsting for gore."

Ski clubs evolved at the same time. There was the Gunnison County Snowshoe Club, which organized a meeting with special trains, 2,000 attendees, and races with prize money. Ouray had its Mount Sneffles Snowshoe Club. And there were "Ladies Races," which a few observers perceived as somewhat dangerous to the social mores of Victorian America. But photographers took innumerable photographs of women and men poised and balanced on skis in several mountain towns. The social fabric did not fall apart.

As the 19th century waned, the railroad, stagecoach, and sleigh did away with most of the uses of skis for work, but the sporting events and festivals built around skis led to a more formalized sport as the 20th century dawned. Ski clubs had emerged in Denver and elsewhere. Many outdoor clubs engaged in ski activities as part of their overall goals. The Colorado Mountain Club, formed in 1912, was one of the first organizations to pick up on the new fancy. In 1915, three years after its founding, the club held its first ski outing to Fern Lake Lodge, near Estes Park, which became the site of many memorable winter outings.[3]

Ski Sailing. This Barnum & Bailey circus poster depicts Carl Howelsen "ski sailing," as early ski jumping was known.

Skiing for sport in Colorado got a tremendous boost through the work of Carl Howelsen, a cross-country and ski-jumping champion in the evolving sport in Europe. An immigrant from Norway, and a stonemason and bricklayer by trade, he came to Colorado in 1909, founded ski clubs in Denver, and worked on building ski jumps, where he and his cohorts drew acclaim. It was a "spectacle," noted the *Denver Post*; a "novelty," said others; and a drama as if "shot with bullet-like speed ... negotiating great distances," said a third commentator. In 1921, Howelsen's efforts prompted the National Ski Association to hold its first national championships in the West in Colorado, where crowds estimated to be from 40,000 to 50,000 enjoyed the events. Howelsen won the championship.

By then, however, he had relocated again, this time to the mountains at Hot Sulphur Springs. Here, he established a winter carnival. At the event, he met Marjorie Perry, a mine owner's daughter originally from Denver and an early member of the Colorado Mountain Club. Perry persuaded Howelsen to move to Steamboat Springs, where he found the dry, deep snow to his liking and established a ski-jumping center on what eventually

became Howelsen Hill. Everywhere he went, Howelsen trained skiers, organized ski clubs, developed winter carnivals, and promoted skiing as a recreational sport. But Steamboat Springs remained a major skiing center. There, remembered Perry, kids even practiced skiing off the roofs of their homes, so deep was the snow in that era.

By the time Howelsen returned to Norway in the early 1920s, he and others had established skiing as a sport for both men and women. Steamboat Springs would eventually produce more American Olympic skiers than any other community in the United States.[4]

The interwar years saw important changes in skiing. In 1920s Europe, skiing technology made significant advances, notably in Austria with the advent of shorter skis, the use of two poles to replace one, and quicker turning styles, the result of which was the evolution of downhill or alpine skiing. In the 1930s, the popularity of

PIONEERS IN SKIING

Henry Buchtel (1906–1988). Henry Buchtel, grandson of the Colorado governor by the same name, joined the Colorado Mountain Club while a teenager and quickly became an avid skier and mountaineer. In 1951, he was co-leader of the first climbing party to ascend Mount McKinley (Denali) via what is now called the West Buttress route. The team included Bradford Washburn, who headed the Boston Museum of Science, along with Colorado Mountain Club members Barry Bishop, John Ambler, Mel Griffiths, and Terry Moore.

A physician like his father, Buchtel and his wife had four children. Despite his busy life, however, he devoted much of his leisure time to leading club outings and serving as editor of the club's monthly publication, *Trail & Timberline*, for which he also wrote articles. In one, "Skiing before Emily Post," published in January 1939, Buchtel remembered early cross-country skiing. "We all had our special secret formulas for ski wax," he said. "As I recall, mine was six parts paraffin to four parts beeswax with one drop of oil of coriander and a dash of paprika. (I may have confused this with my gin recipe but no matter.) The wax was no good anyway."

Henry Buchtel. Sporting lederhosen, Buchtel represents the European fashion of his day. Though seen on occasion, such European dress never caught on among American mountaineers.

Courtesy of Colorado Mountain Club Archives.

Ski Tracks in the Rockies. High above timberline, the broken trail in nearly pristine snow celebrates a party of skiers out for a day in the high country.

Photograph by Christopher J. Case. Courtesy of Christopher J. Case.

skiing grew dramatically in both Europe and the United States, a reflection of a new interest in the outdoors generally by the employed and the well-to-do who had largely escaped the ravages of the Great Depression. American ski clubs brought in European instructors, along with the glamour they represented, and skiing became a fashionable sport at elite eastern colleges. The rise of the Nazis and their takeover of Austria divided ski schools politically, one result of which was that many anti-Nazi Austrians left for the United States and other countries.

These developments gradually affected skiing in Colorado. The new downhill techniques, while proliferating in the Northeast, came west as early as 1923, when one Marquis "Bend More the Knee" Albizzi revolutionized downhill skiing by teaching enthusiasts in the Colorado Mountain Club the Austrian downhill techniques. Other European instructors followed—so many from such a variety of countries that one resident of Climax remembered he "learned how to snowplow and counterstem in seven different languages."

Another key to skiing's development in Colorado was the Arlberg Club. It evolved when Graeme McGowan, described as "a gentleman skier from Denver," discovered the skiing potential at the West Portal of the newly constructed Moffat Tunnel and built a small lodge there for himself and his friends, all members of the Colorado Mountain Club. The Arlberg group took the name from a popular new style of skiing in Europe—downhill skiing—partly invented and certainly popularized by Hannes Schneider of St. Anton am Arlberg in Austria. Taking advantage of developments pioneered by ski troops in World War I, Schneider combined the snowshoe turn or half snowshoe with stem to replace the telemark turn. He used two poles and shorter, narrower, more maneuverable, and faster skis in his Arlberg system, which he popularized in the 1920s. The purpose of the Arlberg Club was "to encourage the development of downhill skiing in Colorado." Weekend trips to the lodge and the sponsorship of downhill and slalom races beginning in 1929 enhanced the sport statewide and popularized Winter Park as an important ski area. CMC members soon launched ski clubs at

Lookout Mountain, Berthoud Pass, and other places on the Front Range. McGowan, a consultant to the US Forest Service, turned a service building into a clubhouse, bought a placer mining claim known as Mary Jane, and created Portal Resorts.

In the later 1930s, Andre Roch, a Swiss skier, began developing the resort town of Aspen, then a mostly abandoned mining town. Its first trails were perilous. Elizabeth Paepcke remembered how her ski party got down the mountain: "It snowed silently as we followed the faint outlines of a logging road through forests broken by outcroppings of rock and an occasional meadow. When we came to a steep bank of snow, our guide proceeded alone testing every step with his ski pole." The group had to wait and watch. "Only after crossing safely himself were we allowed to make the traverse, one by one. No one spoke or made the slightest noise in fear that the vibration of a voice should send us and the entire mass avalanching down the mountainside." But skiing at Aspen took hold, and the Roch Run on Aspen Mountain quickly became one of the nation's most celebrated ski trails.

Despite these European initiatives, which led to the rise of alpine skiing, neither cross-country skiing nor ski jumping died out in Colorado. In the mountains, people continued to ski for recreation in isolated areas. At Gunnison, Western State College developed the collegiate sport in the 1910s. Skiers there sometimes took the train to Quicks Hill at Crested Butte to ski. Winter carnivals along the Front Range promoted ski jumping and cross-country skiing in the mountains west of Denver and as far northwest as Steamboat Springs. And in 1928, out of the Colorado Mountain Club evolved the Arlberg Ski Club, as mentioned earlier, the state's first club devoted specifically to downhill skiing. The idea of a new club originated on the train ride back through the new Moffat Tunnel after a day on the fine downhill terrain at West Portal near the entrance to Middle Park. There, the Arlberg members developed a clubhouse and the next year began to promote downhill and slalom skiing. Clubs and carnivals grew in number and popularity in the 1930s, despite the Great Depression, and in 1941, Aspen hosted the National Championships.

Still, as downhill skiing grew in popularity, two central problems continued: how to get to ski areas, such as they were, and once there, how to get up the mountains. In the 1920s and 1930s, most roads through the mountains were unpaved trails and wagon roads, although that was slowly changing. Many counties and the state itself began paving roads in the mountains, and in the late 1930s, Charles Vail and the Colorado Highway Department opened Vail Pass, the first real road across the central Rockies directly west of Denver. And in the late 1930s, the Ski Train from Denver evolved, particularly with the creation of Winter Park at West Portal as part of the Denver Mountain Park system.

But for alpine skiers, getting up the mountains remained a problem, although improvements were coming in that regard, as well. Aspen evolved its famous—some would say infamous—boat tow, which used two sleds to the second largest ski area in Colorado, and then was introduced, to much more fanfare, at Aspen, where the skiers swathed in blankets rode the "fast" single, heavy iron chair at glacial speeds to reach the summit, their bottoms invariably frozen to the seat.[5]

World War II was a watershed for skiing in Colorado. In the winter of 1939/1940, a group of Bostonians, savoring a few martinis, talked about how successful Finnish troops had been in holding off far larger Soviet armies, and they

Winter Park Skiers and Boat Tow, 1942. For downhill skiers, getting up the mountain was a problem. Some early ski areas tried to solve the problem with a boat tow, a device that eventually gave way to the poma lift, the T-bar, the chairlift, and a few gondolas.

Photograph by Otto Roach. Courtesy of Roach Photos–Gallery Roach, Denver.

A Soldier in the 10th Mountain Division. The most famous military unit to train in Colorado during World War II, the division pioneered new techniques and equipment while training at Camp Hale, Leadville, Aspen, and other venues. It later distinguished itself on the Italian front. Some 10th Mountain veterans became key figures in the postwar American ski industry.

Courtesy of Denver Public Library.

carry skiers partway up Aspen Mountain. Winter Park tried a J-bar, a mechanism that evolved into the T-bar. The Poma lift made its appearance, as did the rope tow. All of these technologies had their place in the expanding sport, but the boat tow was a technological dead end, while the others continued to be used for decades. The best answer to the uphill problem was the chairlift. Based on the aerial tramway used in mining for decades, the single-chair apparatus made its appearance first at Berthoud Pass, once feared that the United States was likely to enter the war at some point. That very night, Minot "Minnie" Dole, president of the National Ski Patrol, and Roger Langley, president of the National Ski Association, decided to petition the secretary of war to create a unit trained in winter and mountainous warfare if such troops were ever needed in defending the United States. Ultimately, this suggestion led to the creation of the 87th Infantry Regiment, the first of three that would make up the 10th Mountain Division. The National Ski Patrol was designated to interview and recruit troops—"the only infantry division in history to ever require an interview to join," quipped one veteran many years later.

Ultimately, in 1942, the army chose Pando, Colorado, as the base of the division's training. This location, barely a whistle-stop, had important transportation linkages. Pando was on the Denver and Rio Grande Western Railroad, on a new road over Tennessee Pass to Leadville, and near the new road over Vail Pass to Denver. The 10th Mountain Division drew recruits from many countries and many parts of the United States—the bulk of them with some sort of ski or outdoor background. And in late 1942, Camp Hale—"Camp Hell," said some—became the division's base of operations. As training went forward, many soldiers came to appreciate the snow and terrain for superb skiing. Others noted the wealthy tourists and cheap land. Still more noticed nearly abandoned mining towns adjacent to fine ski terrain. The 10th Mountain Division went on to distinguish itself on the Italian front, and once the war ended, some of these troops came home to launch a new, different postwar ski industry, especially in Colorado.

Aspen was a natural magnet—it had hosted alpine games before the war, real estate was inexpensive, buildings were available, and new entrepreneurs could capitalize on the famous Roch Run. Tenth

Ski Broadmoor. An Austrian-born refugee from Nazi Germany, exiled as the result of his "degenerate art," Herbert Bayer helped introduce Bauhaus art and design to the United States, a modernist movement that combined art, architecture, and design to enhance lifestyles. This whimsical poster advertised one of many Front Range ski areas that disappeared owing largely to lack of snow in a global warming era.

Poster by Herbert Bayer. Courtesy of Hubert Bayer Collection and Archives, Denver Art Museum and © 2010 Artists Rights Society (ARS), New York/VG Bild-Sunst, Bonn.

Mountain veterans soon became key players in the dramatic expansion of prewar areas like Arapahoe Basin and Winter Park, and they launched new areas such as Loveland, Breckenridge, and especially Vail. Ultimately, they would turn the postwar ski industry from a small, local, club-like background into one that emphasized the destination resort.[6]

The development of the interstate highway system also had a huge impact on downhill skiing. Construction of highways in the 1950s and later meant fast transportation west to Loveland Pass. There, the bottleneck began when skiers had to take to the old two-lane road over the divide, and the

Keystone Poster. Gene Hoffmann designed this poster to advertise the Keystone ski area, which was developed at the site of an old mining area, as were a number of other resorts.

Poster by Gene Hoffman. Courtesy of Susan Tangate.

PIONEERS IN SKIING

Pete Siebert (1924–2002). A native of Massachusetts, Pete Siebert (pronounced Cy-bert) served in the 10th Mountain Division in World War II. Badly wounded in Italy and told he would never ski again, he returned to Colorado after the war, recovered from his injuries, and later qualified for the US Ski Team. After working at various ski areas, he and a group of partners, organized as the Trans Montane Rod and Gun Club, quietly acquired lands in the Eagle Valley to create "the most beautiful ski resort in the world." Construction began on land between Eagle and Vail Pass, and the Vail Ski Resort opened with two chairlifts in December 1962. Vail evolved into the largest and one of the most popular ski areas in the United States— its popularity fostered by controlled Bavarian style design coupled with superb snow and terrain. Siebert and his partners envisioned and promulgated a unity of town development and slope development with design guidelines that provided a coherent image that many other resorts lacked. They also hoped that Vail would become the centerpiece of the 1976 Olympics until the voters thought otherwise.

Pete Siebert. Shown here on the slopes, Siebert, a veteran of the 10th Mountain Division, was a key figure in the development of the Vail ski area, which became one of the largest resorts in the world.

Courtesy of Vail Ski Museum.

Buddy Werner. Werner led the way in American alpine racing for a decade. "We've got a program . . . that's on a par with the Europeans," he proclaimed.

Photograph by Richard Frischauf.

advent of the underpowered Volkswagen Beetle slowed passage even more. But once across Loveland Pass, skiers had quick access to the central Rockies, and new areas—Keystone, Breckenridge, Vail, and eventually Beaver Creek— developed on that corridor. The interstate system provided faster access to even more distant Aspen and Steamboat Springs.

Lift technology progressed in scale and speed. The J-bar, T-bar, and rope tow remained, but only for marginal use in special circumstances. Gondolas appeared in a number of areas—notably Aspen, Vail, and Steamboat Springs—but the greatest advances came with chair technology. It soared. The slow, one-seat iron chair that froze occupants to the seat gave way to the double chair, the triple chair, the quadruple chair, and finally in the 1990s the high-speed quad lift, which whisked people up-mountain with unprecedented speed and relative comfort. It solved the problem of standing in

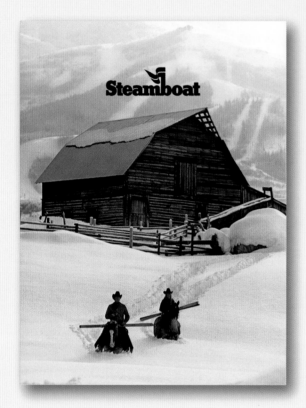

Steamboat Springs Barn Poster. This memorable poster linked the deep snow of Steamboat Springs with the cultural icon represented by the American cowboy.

Courtesy of Steamboat Ski and Resort Corporation.

45-minute lift lines on weekends, but it crowded hundreds of people on the downhill side. Solving one problem created another.

An additional problem on the slopes evolved with the rise of snowboards in the late 1980s and their surge in popularity in the 1990s. Tensions immediately arose between skiers and boarders, and many ski resorts kept boarders off the lifts and, in essence, off the slopes. But the surging popularity of snowboards among younger enthusiasts made one ski resort after another eliminate their restrictions. In the early 21st century, Aspen became the final resort to cave in.

Ski resorts also had to contend with the ironic problem of not enough snow in dry years. The result was a reliance on snow-making machinery that created snowstorms on sunny days and allowed lifts to open ever earlier in the season—a trend that became a popular contest between resorts.

The dramatic success of alpine skiing drove both cross-country skiing and ski jumping into the background in the postwar years, but the powerful advance of downhill skiing as both major sport and component of the economy drew opposition in various forms. Some of this animosity was driven by the growing cost of the sport, its popularity, and the increasing emphasis on destination ski resorts. Other aspects of opposition reflected the larger concerns of some groups in the environmental movement.

As downhill skiing, the winter sport of baby boomers, became a key driver in the booming postwar economy, in the late 1960s city officials sought to bring the 1976 Winter Olympics to Denver to highlight the city, the state, and the mountains and to promote further growth. An energetic campaign persuaded the International Olympic Committee to award Denver the 1976 games. Skating events would be held in the Mile High City, cross-country skiing on trails to be built around Evergreen, and downhill racing at the ski resorts farther west. But the promoters had dramatically underestimated costs and neglected public sentiment when they went to the state legislature for funding, and they had also ignored the growing environmental movement that focused on slower growth in Colorado. A referendum went on the state ballot in 1972, and when voters, by a 3-to-2 margin, opposed public funding for the games, Denver relinquished the award. It was just as well. Little snow fell in 1976, which might have hurt, rather than benefited, the industry and the pro-growth movement. The anti-Olympics campaign also helped secure the reputation of a then-obscure state legislator, CMC member Richard D. Lamm, who leveraged his successful anti-Olympics stance into a successful bid for the governor's office in November 1974.

While downhill skiing had turned into a well-to-do, destination resort business by the 1970s, a backlash to these developments emerged, coupled with the rise of the environmental movement and its interest in preserving wilderness areas. That momentum gave a new push to largely forgotten cross-country skiing. Once a sport of long, thick skis and a balance pole, it acquired some of the features of downhill skiing—shorter, lighter skis and twin poles made largely by Scandinavian manufacturers—and it grew in popularity with the increasing interest in Olympic cross-country events. The sport flourished in the 1970s. In a sense, skiing in Colorado had come full circle from pioneer days.

The new cross-country skiing had wide appeal. If alpine skiing offered breathtaking summit views and exciting downhill runs, cross-country skiing provided a more leisurely pace; a more peaceful aesthetic experience in the woods, lakes, and valleys; and the thrills of downhill runs on narrow trails with rocks, trees, branches, and stumps

1976 Winter Olympics Poster. Gene Hoffman designed this pro-Olympics ski poster for the proposed 1976 games in Colorado, only to have the voters reject public funding for the event and end the dreams of its proponents.

Poster by Gene Hoffman. Courtesy of the collection of Richard Lamm.

Beaver Creek. Though famous for her Denver street scenes, Barbara Froula also captured mountain towns old and new in her characteristic style. Here, she portrays Beaver Creek, a destination resort created by the expansion of Vail.

Painting by Barbara Froula. Private Collection.

dead ahead. And it was a far less expensive sport than alpine skiing. Skiers could outfit themselves completely for a fraction of the cost of alpine equipment. Hiking trails in the summer gave way to ski trails in the winter. Some mountain golf courses found a winter business, ski areas designed for cross-country enthusiasts made their own appearance, and restaurants deep in the woods found a winter clientele. Old mining towns like Leadville created cross-country trails through ruins, and even major ski areas offered cross-country terrain as a sideline. Some skiers refused to pay for lift tickets and simply skied up the mountains—which were generally public domain—and skied down using the old telemark turn unknown to alpine enthusiasts. And to shelter skiers in the backcountry, some organizations built cabins and what were known as yurts, simple structures based on the huts of herders in Asia. Yurt systems deep in the woods could be rented, and the development of the 10th Mountain Division system of remote huts provided additional shelter for those out for several days.

Like cross-country skiing itself, the use of huts and yurts was nothing new. They came with recreational skiing, and the Boulder Hut of the Colorado Mountain Club, built in 1928, remained in use well into the 21st century. But it was Alfred (Fred) Braun, a Club member from Aspen, who began Colorado's modern hut system. Born in Germany, he moved from Chicago to Aspen, where he and his wife operated a ski lodge. In conjunction with the US Ski Association, he built and managed five huts accessible from nearby Ashcroft and was instrumental in starting Aspen Mountain Rescue and its first ambulance service. Braun's hut ideas spread to other ski areas and influenced the development of the 10th Mountain system, spearheaded by Aspen architect Fritz Benedict (brother-in-law of the famous Bauhaus artist/architect Herbert Bayer).

HIGH ALTITUDE PULMONARY EDEMA

Alex Drummond (1937–) and **Charles Houston** (1913–2009). In late December 1958, Alex Drummond returned to Colorado from San Francisco, where he had visited his mother. A few days later, Drummond and Pat Caywood embarked on an epic ski tour in the Maroon Bells area near Aspen. The trip was to celebrate Alex's 21st birthday by skiing up the Maroon Creek Valley, crossing 12,420-foot Buckskin Pass, and continuing north to Snowmass Lake, from which they would attempt to ski/climb 14,092-foot Snowmass Mountain.

Early on, however, Drummond became strangely weak and slow. By the third day, he was coughing a lot, gasping for breath, and raving at night. Caywood realized he had to get help. So, after giving Drummond his own sleeping bag and pad, he left him in the tent and skied 12 miles down the valley to Snowmass Falls Ranch.

By telephone he reached Dr. Charles Houston, an Aspen physician who was also an exceptional mountaineer. Although it was New Year's Eve, Houston rounded up a rescue team. The next day, they skied to Drummond and hauled him out on a sled. By 9:00 that night, he was in the hospital, resting comfortably. Eventually, he made a complete recovery. But what had he recovered from? Pneumonia? Acute heart failure? Drummond's mother suggested that his problems were related to his going to high altitude too soon after having been at sea level.

For the next year and a half, Houston consulted with some of the country's preeminent physicians, trying to come up with answers. In September 1960, he published an article in the *New England Journal of Medicine* titled "Acute Pulmonary Edema of High Altitude." Although it turned out that several years earlier, Peruvian physicians had published a similar article in Spanish, it is Houston's article, written in English, that is credited with launching a worldwide awareness of the effects of high altitude on humans.

Houston's chance encounter with Alex Drummond changed the focus of his life. After working for the Peace Corps in India and Washington, D.C., he directed the High Altitude Physiology Laboratory, located at 17,500 feet on Canada's Mount Logan. Because he wrote and lectured so extensively about the effects of high altitude on humans, he came to be called "the father of high altitude physiology." Houston died in 2009 at the age of 96. The Altitude Research Center at the University of Colorado School of Medicine has named an endowed chair in his honor.

For 20 years, Drummond was public relations director at the National Center for Atmospheric Research. He wrote a widely read biography, *Enos Mills: Citizen of Nature*.

Alex Drummond. Drummond posed for the camera at Forest Lake near the East Portal on his 70th birthday. An accomplished skier, in 1978, he and two friends were the first to ski across Colorado. They began their epic 490-mile journey on March 19 near Durango and arrived at Chambers Lake, near Fort Collins, on May 3.

Courtesy of Alex Drummond.

Charles Houston, MD. The dramatic rescue of Alex Drummond on New Year's Day 1959 launched Houston on a quest to study the effects of high altitude on humans. He came to be known as "the father of high altitude physiology."

Photo by Tom Hornbein. Courtesy of Tom Hornbein.

Fred Braun. Aspenite Fred Braun started the state's first hut system.   Photograph by David Hiser. Courtesy of David Hiser.

Taggert Hut. This hut, with a nice view of Castle Creek, is off the Ashcroft Trailhead near Aspen.

Photograph by David Hiser. Courtesy of David Hiser.

Skiers Leaving Margy's Hut. Built in 1982, Margy's Hut, funded by former Secretary of Defense Robert McNamara, was one of the first two huts built in the 10th Mountain Division system of 20 cabins. McNamara financed the shelter as a memorial to his wife, Margy.

Photograph by David Hiser. Courtesy of David Hiser.

Like everything else, cross-country skiing underwent technological development. The early waxable skis gave way to plastic skis, from which waxless, fish-scale skis for the uphill climb evolved. Thin and clumsy when they first appeared, they became ever more sturdy and stream-lined as they largely supplanted the wooden ski. Bindings became more sophisticated, as the once-standard three-pin system gave way to tech-nologies that used some of the features of the stiff alpine boot to provide better maneuverability downhill. New clothing proliferated. And the price of the sport rose substantially by the end of the 20th century, but it still remained far less expensive than downhilling.

The century's end saw a convergence of cross-country and down-hill skiing in so-called extreme skiing. Newly designed, sophisticated skis and bindings made it possible for bold, daring skiers seeking greater challenges and thrills to ski higher than the lifts would take them. Downhill areas like Crested Butte added steep, rocky, double-diamond runs accessible only by skiing or climbing up. And new technology enabled others to ski and climb to the top of Colorado's highest peaks, an activity once the sole domain of intrepid winter mountaineers, and then convert their skis to good downhill equipment to descend from the summits of Thirteeners and Fourteeners.

Economic growth in the mountains, a result of the ski industry, also became a public concern. In the later 20th century, many ski areas met strong opposition when they sought to expand extant terrain, develop adjacent mountains, and promote business and home construction. Many Coloradans had serious reservations about continued growth along the I-70 corridor—a development that had jammed the slopes, created traffic tie-ups, turned tiny communities into sprawling mountain suburbs, and added to noise and pollution, all of which seemed to defeat the aesthetics of skiing. Federal agencies on whose

Skiers on the Rocks. A group of spring skiers takes a siesta from the ardors of wine and cross-country skiing at East Portal.

Photograph by Janet N. Robertson. Courtesy of Janet N. Robertson.

Snowshoers at Isabelle Lake. Apache Peak (left) and Shoshoni Peak (left center) form a breathtaking backdrop as this party of snowshoers forges ahead in the Indian Peaks Wilderness Area.

Photograph by Christopher J. Case. Courtesy of Christopher J. Case.

Steamboat Springs Winter Carnival, 1955.
Music, recreation, and outdoor festivals coalesced into one form of mountain activity in 20th-century Colorado. Here, a "marching" band skis through Steamboat Springs in the course of a February festival in the mountains.

Photograph by Otto Roach. Courtesy of Roach Photos–Gallery Roach, Denver.

lands skiing took place found themselves caught in the middle. The controversies worked themselves out through appropriate channels, but the resolutions were not acceptable for some. In 1998 a group of radical environmentalists in the Earth Liberation Front set fire to Vail's famous Two Elk Lodge near the mountain summit in a brazen night attack, a crime that went unsolved for years and was said to be the worst example of ecoterrorism in the nation's history. Vail rebuilt the lodge.

But by the early 21st century, skiing focused on the high country had become a central part of life in Colorado. The small individual operations had evolved into a few large corporations. Global warming and quick access to the mountains had largely ended skiing on the high plains and drove activity to the resorts and terrain of the I-70 corridor west of Denver. And if alpine skiing, coupled with the surging popularity of snowboarding, dominated the sport, cross-country skiing enjoyed a powerful resurgence that took enthusiasts deep into the backcountry. Extreme skiing had emerged to challenge the boldest—the daredevils if you will—on the steepest trails and highest mountains. But no one appeared to have revitalized train jumping in the tradition of Andy Bray.

Extreme Skier. This image shows Matt Kamper ascending the high ridge on Capitol Peak. In the late 20th century, as skiers and mountaineers challenged their abilities ever more, they turned to what became known as extreme skiing, one goal of which was to climb and ski down all of the Fourteeners. In the case of very difficult mountains like Capitol Peak, skiers rappelled down as necessary before putting on their skis.

Photograph by Jarrett Luttrell. Courtesy of Jarrett Luttrell.

Emerald View. Hallett Peak rises over Emerald Lake on a blustery winter day in Rocky Mountain National Park. Painting by James Disney. Courtesy of James Disney.

Above Jim and Dianne's House. Among the most important painters of the late 20th and early 21st centuries, Joellyn Duesberry makes use of intense colors and geometry in her art in interpreting vast landscapes. Colorado's mountains have been a key theme in her diverse work over the years.

Painting by Joellyn Duesberry.
Courtesy of Joellyn Duesberry.

CHAPTER 6

PAINTING THE PEAKS

JAMES E. FELL, JR.

*When I moved west ... the arid sculptural light of the western
landscape jolted me into a new language of quirky forms and
colors unlike any prior stimulus from former humid eastern
landscapes where everything has shared edges. It was as if a veil
had been lifted to reveal abstract geometric nature.*

—JOELLYN DUESBERRY

Like mountaineering itself, art in Colorado evolved in times very distant from our own. Ancient peoples depicted what are clearly mountains on the pottery, pictographs, and petroglyphs that have survived, and they probably did so on other media now long lost. Collectively, these images suggest the importance of the mountains in the ancient cultures of the region.

The modern art of the mountains emerged with the coming of European explorers, notably the Spanish, and with them art and mapmaking went hand in hand. The famous Miera y Pacheco map of the late 18th century is clearly both art and map as it depicts the mountains and rivers of Utah and Colorado, a reflection of how explorers sought to meld both mapmaking and art in an age before the rise of photography.

The first American images of the Rocky Mountains emerged in the age of early 19th-century exploration—a time when art, exploration, and naturalism served as accompaniments to each other. The initial American explorers who pushed their way through the mountains were Meriwether Lewis and William Clark, who crossed the northern Rockies on their celebrated journey of 1804–1806, and Zebulon Pike, who passed through the central and southern Rockies in 1806–1807. Although both parties explored simultaneously, neither produced any images of the region. But Pike's published report, and rumors about

KEY PAINTERS

Charles Partridge Adams (1859–1939). The art of Charles Partridge Adams reflected the larger traditions of the Hudson River School, although most of his work came well after its heyday and thus elitist art critiques are often dismissive of his talent. A student of Helen Henderson Chain, a mountaineer himself, and a founder of the Colorado Mountain Club, he painted the mountains, lakes, and valleys of the entire state in a career that evolved from the early 1870s until health issues forced him to resettle in California in the 1920s.

KEY PAINTERS

George Elbert Burr (1858–1932). George Burr came to Denver in midcareer, probably for health reasons. Born in Monroe Falls, Ohio, he received his initial art training from his mother, studied briefly at the Art Institute of Chicago, then began his career as an illustrator for national magazines. He later traveled, studied, and painted in Europe. Relocating to Denver in 1906, he hiked through the mountains, becoming a prolific creator of etchings of the Southwest and a painter of the Rockies. His wife, Elizabeth Rogers Burr, was a charter member of the Colorado Mountain Club.

the unpublished Lewis and Clark account, created a demand for them that was filled by later expeditions and so gave rise to the mountains as subjects for artists.

The first of these explorations entering modern-day Colorado was the Yellow Stone Expedition, led by Major Stephen Harriman Long of the US Army. This reconnaissance developed in 1819 out of a huge military expedition designed to build an immense post on the Yellow Stone River in present-day Montana. But in the hard times following the Panic of 1819, Congress slashed funding for the post and instead decided to turn Long's advance party into one engaged in scientific exploration. The group would cross the high plains to explore the Rocky Mountains and find the Grand Peak, which Zebulon Pike had described some years before. As a result, Long was recalled from his advanced post at Engineer Cantonment near Council Bluffs in modern-day Iowa and sent to Philadelphia to hire a scientist to assess the region and two artists to paint the landscape. The scientist engaged was Edwin James. The artists hired were Titian Ramsey Peale and Samuel Seymour.

Once back at Engineer Cantonment, Long and his comrades struck west across the plains. They followed the Platte River, then the South Platte; near modern-day Fort Morgan, Colorado, they sighted a curious phenomenon on the western horizon—a small blue cloud that didn't move. As they continued west, the small blue cloud turned into an immense mountain that the men concluded must be the Grand Peak described by Pike. To confirm this, they traced the Big Thompson River west, but after a time the group concluded that this was not the great peak described by Pike. Even so, Long decided to name the mountain James Peak, after his scientist, but the name was not to stick.

The party headed south down the Front Range, taking careful

Pikes Peak in the Rain. Because there were no known images of the Rocky Mountains, the federal government hired two artists, Titian Peale and Samuel Seymour, to participate in the Long Expedition of 1820. This work, by Seymour, is the oldest known painting of Pikes Peak, which members of the expedition climbed that year in the first known ascent of the mountain.

Painting by Samuel Seymour. Courtesy of Boston Museum of Fine Arts.

observations as it went, with Peale and Seymour drawing and painting the plains and mountains. They depicted the flowers and animals of the region such as elk and buffalo, they painted Indians on horseback—and they captured the mountains: Longs Peak, the Indian Peaks, even the Flatirons rising above the future city of Boulder. Farther south, they captured the South Platte River flowing out of the mountains onto the high plains, and as they moved ever farther south, they could see the outline of another peak rising in the mist—the great mountain described by Pike. At its base, Peale painted what became known as the Garden of the Gods, and Seymour made a sketch for what became "Pikes Peak in the Rain," the oldest known image of the famous peak. At the same time, James led a small group to the summit, the first known ascent of the mountain. From there, the expedition continued south to the Arkansas River before turning east to return to "the states." The images of Seymour and Peale, displayed one time before making their way into public and private collections, were the first of the Rocky Mountains that the American public saw. Some graced the pages of the *Long Report*, which appeared in 1823 (a report that also characterized the Great Plains as the "Great American Desert").

In the years that followed, many expeditions hired artists who sketched and painted and whose work appeared in the reports of their expeditions. Lieutenant J. W. Abert, who explored the region in the mid-1840s, was one of the best of these artists. Another of note was Richard Kern, who traveled west with several expeditions. It was Kern

who captured Pikes Peak from what is now downtown Colorado Springs, along with various passes in the Rockies and other scenes before he was killed on the Gunnison Expedition of 1853. By the time of the Pikes Peak Gold Rush of 1859, some 40 years of sketching and painting had left behind a considerable pictorial record of the region.

As the gold rush unfolded in 1859 and after, so, too, did the art of the mountains. The first images came largely from artists visiting the region to see and paint the mountains, and then leave to complete their works elsewhere. The work of many individuals reflected the earlier utilitarian tradition of the explorers, but others brought to the Rocky Mountains the important artistic traditions of the era. The utilitarian now accompanied mainstream painting.

Early on, the most important of these traditions was the Hudson River School. Originating in the East, and powerfully influenced by German art and German romanticism, it became a large local, then regional, school in Jacksonian America, circa 1825 to 1848. It reflected three themes consistent with the expanding republic of that era: discovery, exploration, and settlement; within those themes, its painters emphasized dramatic natural settings in which people and nature existed in harmony. The paintings claimed to be realistic, though the artists often idealized their interpretations of landscape, and they sometimes reflected the view that the wildness and grandeur of the landscape were a manifestation of God. Its first artists, notably Thomas Cole, focused on the East, but

Longs Peak from Denver. One of Colorado's earliest painters, Thomas Worthington Whittredge interpreted many areas along the Front Range and in Estes Park through the Hudson River style, which achieved its greatest flowering in dramatic paintings of the American West.

Painting by Thomas Worthington Whittredge. Courtesy of Buffalo Bill Historical Center.

Timberline Austerities.
The first director of the Broadmoor Art Academy, John F. Carlson created art that depicted Colorado with a focus on the Pikes Peak region.

Painting by John F. Carlson.
Courtesy of Dusty and Kathy Loo
Historic Colorado Collection.

later painters, the so-called second generation, headed west. One goal they had, in the wake of the gold rush, was "Pikes Peak," the early generic name for the region—meaning Denver, the Front Range, and the mountains immediately to the west.

Early artists heading to the Rockies included Thomas Worthington Whittredge and John F. Kensett. Both eastern and European trained, they traveled to Colorado on one or more trips in the 1860s, and from these journeys emerged notable paintings of the Front Range, especially those by the remarkable Whittredge, whose works dramatically depicted the plains, the rivers, and the first settlers dwarfed by the larger mountain landscape in the background.

Other, deemed by many to be more important, members of the Hudson River School in Colorado included Albert Bierstadt and Thomas Moran. Bierstadt combined both the more stylized, utilitarian tradition of the early explorers and the Hudson River School itself. In the 1850s he served as a federal survey artist in what is now Colorado and Wyoming, as well as elsewhere, and he returned in the 1860s and 1870s to capture the drama of the region, especially in his paintings of Longs Peak, Estes Park, and the Mount Evans area. Eventually, Mount Bierstadt would be named for him. His counterpart, Thomas Moran, made his first journey to Colorado as part of the Hayden Survey in 1874. He made many subsequent trips to study, climb, and paint, and, like Bierstadt, he left behind a number of major paintings of the region, including his now famous "Mountain of the Holy Cross."

Some painters in this school made Colorado their

Estes Park. Arguably the greatest painter of the Hudson River School, which sought to capture the hand of God on the American landscape, Albert Bierstadt summoned all of his talent and energy in creating this inspiring image of Longs Peak. It remains one of his most famous paintings. The Twin Sisters rises to the left, with Longs Peak center right.

Painting by Albert Bierstadt. Courtesy of Denver Public Library.

permanent home. Among the first was Helen Henderson Chain. A native of Indianapolis, she and her husband settled in Denver in the early 1870s, where he became a partner in the Chain and Hardy Book Store. It became something of an early art center, where she and others sold their work. The Chains often camped in the mountains, and a chance meeting with the painter Hamilton Hamilton (yes, he had the same first and last name) spurred her art. Her most famous painting is her "Mountain of the Holy Cross," done from almost the same location as the more famous one by Moran. She later became the first woman known to have painted the Grand Canyon, but her career was cut short when she and her husband drowned when their ship foundered while on a trip to East Asia.

Chain's most famous student was Charles Partridge Adams, Colorado's best known artist of the late 19th and early 20th century. Born in Franklin, Massachusetts, he came west in the 1870s when his mother decided to bring the family to Denver in hope that the dry air would improve the family's health—at least one family member had tuberculosis. Adams worked in the Chain and Hardy Book Store, where Helen Chain encouraged his painting. He camped and climbed in the mountains and exhibited his work with Bierstadt, Moran, and other members of the Hudson River School, particularly at the National Mining and Industrial Exposition sponsored by Colorado mining magnates in 1882. He may have studied with Worthington Whittredge later on. He opened his first studio in Denver in the 1890s but lived mostly in Estes Park and other locales until bad health forced him to relocate to California.

Another key artist in the same tradition was Otis Harvey Young. He went west in the gold rush to California and evolved into an artist there. He eventually came to Colorado, where he became a successful

Helen Henderson Chain. This photograph captures Helen Henderson Chain painting at the easel while in the company of the famous writer, novelist, and crusader for Indian rights, Helen Hunt Jackson.

Unknown Photographer. Courtesy of Denver Public Library.

Mountain of the Holy Cross. One of the first major artists living permanently in Colorado, Helen Henderson Chain exemplified the tenets of the Hudson River School. Until rockfall altered one of the cross ledges, this scene was among the most celebrated in Colorado. Many believed that it literally depicted the hand of God on the landscape, which was a theme central to this school of art.

Painting by Helen Henderson Chain.
Courtesy of Dusty and Kathy Loo Historic Colorado Collection.

Mountain Lake. Artist and mine owner Harvey Otis Young did well in two fields of endeavor in the course of a long career in Colorado and other states before he retired to Colorado Springs. A realist and an impressionist, he captured the grandeur of the Rockies along with innumerable other western settings.

Painting by Harvey Otis Young. Courtesy of Dusty and Kathy Loo Historic Colorado Collection.

mining entrepreneur in Aspen before relocating to Colorado Springs. Like the other artists in the later Hudson River School, he painted all over the West, and his best work reflects a certain mystical quality in his mountain paintings.

As artistic traditions became more complex in the early 20th century, mountains continued to form a central element in the work of most painters coming to Colorado, and this in turn influenced the rise of important regional schools that interpreted the ranges, peaks, and individual mountains in styles particular to the new era. The first to emerge was the Broadmoor Art Academy in Colorado Springs, which was eclectic, if nothing else. In 1919, Spencer and Julia Penrose, founders of the Broadmoor Hotel and backed by a mining fortune, donated their home to help finance the academy's creation. They hired John Fabian Carlson, a Swedish immigrant, to serve as the first director. He was very much a traditionalist in terms of his representational art, although some of his work invoked the ideas of the impressionists of the era. In both styles, he painted dramatic scenes of the Colorado Springs region. But while his own painting tended to emphasize older traditions, he also engaged other artists who were post-impressionist and modernist in their work. This convergence sent Colorado art in a new direction and ultimately led to the founding of the Colorado Springs Fine Arts Center.

A key figure coming to the Broadmoor Art Academy was Birger Sandzen, another Swedish immigrant, who was the head of the Art Department at Bethany College in Lindsborg, Kansas. For some 30 years beginning in 1908, he spent his annual summer holiday in the mountains, first in Colorado Springs and later in Estes Park, where he focused on interpreting the mountains. "I have found some wonderful new sketching grounds—Pike's Peak above timberline," he wrote in 1920. And he used a post-impressionist/modernist style in developing a vast

Garden of the Gods. The famous photographer Laura Gilpin, who lived and worked in Colorado for a time, captured John F. Carlson and his students at the Broadmoor Art Academy painting in the Garden of the Gods.

Photograph by Laura Gilpin. Courtesy of Colorado Springs Fine Arts Center.

number of paintings depicting the Front Range of the Rockies and other venues in bold, bright canvases. Though largely forgotten through the middle years of the century, his reputation as an artist and interpreter of the region reemerged and grew dramatically at the end of the century.

But the most innovative member of the Broadmoor School was Charles Ragland Bunnell. In the course of a long career, he moved from impressionism to cubism to abstraction. His most important works, which arguably make him and Sandzen the two most important artists of the Broadmoor Art Academy, interpret the Pikes Peak region and its mining towns, Cripple Creek and Victor, in cubist style with bold semi-abstract forms and sharply contrasting colors.

The Great Depression of the 1930s created hard times for Colorado artists, as it did for most Americans, but gradually federal programs helped many through employment and purchase. A key figure in the development of such programs was Canadian-born artist George Lawson, best known for his urban paintings of the New York area, which made him one of "The Eight" there, and as an organizer of the both famous and infamous Armory Show of 1913. Later, he became involved with the Broadmoor Art Academy, where he was teaching when the economic crisis struck. Using his New York connections, he proposed to President Franklin Roosevelt a program that evolved into the Federal Arts Project within the Works Progress Administration, the New Deal agency that after 1935 became the largest employer in Depression-ravaged Colorado. His student Bunnell worked for the agency for a time, but he was only one of innumerable artists to do so nationwide.

After World War II, abstract expressionism became the most powerful force in American art. Highbrow elites in the East and elsewhere focused on it as the zenith, the ultimate achievement of the art

Snow and Mountain. A fine reflection of Sandzen's post-impressionist style of broad strokes and bright colors, this painting captures North Arapaho Peak in the Indian Peaks Wilderness Area. A faculty member at Bethany College in Kansas, the Swedish-born Sandzen ventured to Colorado during many summers to capture the landscape and teach at the Broadmoor Art Academy.

Painting by Sven Birger Sandzen. Courtesy of Oscar Thorsen Collection, Birger Sandzen Memorial Gallery, Lindsborg, Kansas.

Cripple Creek Mine. Perhaps the most innovative member of the Broadmoor School, Bunnell departed from the school's emphasis on impressionism to depict the mountains in the new cubist style, which emphasized colors and intersecting planes. The fading mining towns of Cripple Creek and Victor on the west slopes of Pikes Peak, depicted here, comprised an important focus of his work.

Painting by Charles Ragland Bunnell. Courtesy of El Pomar Foundation Permanent Collection.

of Western civilization. While the high peaks remained a central theme of all artists working in Colorado, most postwar students focused their attention here. One result was the end of the Broadmoor Art Academy, which resisted abstraction and failed to find an academic home in the postwar years. And so the focus of Colorado art shifted to Denver. Here, artists like Vance Kirkland and Frank Vavra, who had begun their careers more as post-impressionist artists, moved with the style of the day and became ever more abstract in their work in the postwar years. For "serious" artists, pretty much gone was the representational and even impressionist styles of the early 20th century, at least as far as academic and highbrow art was concerned, although artists like Alfred Wands at Colorado Women's College continued these earlier styles in teaching, painting, and writing.

Yet whatever artistic tradition and style they embraced, most artists of Colorado and the West, while certainly influenced by abstract painting, never fully gave up painting the majesty of the western landscape—its mountains, rivers, deserts, plains, and oceans. Some artists remained rooted in the realist tradition, some continued with impressionism, and many others adapted the ideas of modernism and abstraction to still depict something that actually existed. And so multiple styles came to dominate the works of postwar landscape painters of Colorado who interpreted the mountains as a major theme in their work.

KEY PAINTERS

Charles Ragland Bunnell (1897–1968). If Sven Birger Sandzen was the most famous artist of the Broadmoor School, then Charles Ragland Bunnell was its most innovative. He grew up in Kansas City, Missouri, where he drew on walls and textbooks when he didn't have paper. After serving in the military in World War I, he moved to Colorado Springs, where he studied at the Broadmoor Art Academy and settled down at the base of Pikes Peak, where he used an old boxcar for a studio. His growing interest in using the geometric shapes of modernism clashed both personally and philosophically with the main faculty and realist/impressionist fundamentals of the Broadmoor School. Consequently, he became something of an outsider. But his interest in the mountains, mining, and ruins around the region, captured in spare paintings that depicted hills and mountains as truncated cones, was a remarkable break from the painting tradition of the school and marked a gradual transition to his postwar work, which focused largely on the abstract.

KEY PAINTERS

Vance Kirkland (1904–1981). A graduate of the Cleveland School of Art, Vance Kirkland came to Denver to establish an art department at the University of Denver. Although a clash with the provost cost him his job, Kirkland became one of the leading artists in Denver and eventually returned to the university on his own terms. Early on, he worked in a style that he called "designed realism," more a form of impressionism than anything else—a style that personified a rhythmic movement in rocks, clouds, and other natural wonders. A hiker and climber, he found inspiration in high winds, open spaces above timberline, and mining towns in ruin, and he added antifreeze to paint so that he could work on-site in all temperatures. The mountaineers that appear in some of his work seem caught in a vast landscape far greater than their impact on it. His best landscape art came in the 1920s and 1930s, after which he moved on to abstract work.

Clouds and Mountains. Vance Kirkland painted this landscape as his artistic style was evolving from realism to surrealism, from where it would soon go to abstraction. The founding director of the University of Denver School of Art and a painter with a devilish sense of humor, he once dispatched a student in search of "vanishing points."

Courtesy of Denver Art Museum. Painting by Vance Kirkland Collection; gift of Vance H. and Anne O. Kirkland, 1982.418, and used by permission of Kirkland Museum of Fine & Decorative Art, Denver.

Mountain Climbers. Colorado's most influential mid-20th-century painter, Vance Kirkland drew inspiration from his own mountaineering. Here he captures a group of climbers using rope for safety in their ascent on a hard route. The rock formations around them appear to come alive as creatures fearful of this invasion of their solitude.

Painting by Vance Kirkland.
Courtesy of Kirkland Museum of Fine & Decorative Art, Denver.

Arapahoe Peaks. A founding member of the Colorado Mountain Club, Charles Partridge Adams focused his paintings on the Front Range of the Rockies, although his work encompassed the entire state.

Painting by Charles Partridge Adams. Courtesy of Neil R. Smith Fine Art.

KEY PAINTERS

Frank Vavra (1892–1967). Born in St. Paul, Nebraska, Frank Vavra had few artistic opportunities early in life. He grew up in Nebraska and Wyoming and worked many jobs—one as a window decorator. Wounded in France in World War I, he convalesced in Paris, where he befriended a pupil of the famous French painter Claude Monet. In 1923, Vavra moved to Denver, where he studied at the Denver Art Academy, and married Kathleen H. Huffman, a watercolorist and fashion artist at the Denver Dry Goods Company. In the 1930s and 1940s, he painted impressive landscapes of mountains in Colorado and Wyoming in the realist and impressionist styles. Then in the late 1940s, as abstract painting became so dominant in the art world, he switched to that style. His paintings of the Colorado Rockies remain the hallmark of his career.

Rocky Mountain Landscape. A student of Vance Kirkland, Frank Vavra was a painter whose art moved from realism to abstraction. His mountain landscapes of Colorado and other states form a central component of his early work.

Painting by Frank Vavra.
Courtesy of Dusty and Kathy Loo Historic Colorado Collection.

Spring Saplings. This painting of the Front Range depicts the intense colors and rippling patterns that characterized Eve Drewelowe's later, most important work.

Painting by Eve Drewelowe. Courtesy of Dusty and Kathy Loo Historic Colorado Collection.

KEY PAINTERS

Eve Drewelowe (1899–1989). Born in Iowa, Eve Drewelowe was the first person to graduate from the University of Iowa with a master of fine arts degree. She married a political science student, Jacob van Ek, and the couple moved to Boulder, where he eventually became a dean at the University of Colorado. She helped found the Boulder Artists' Guild and continued to paint, but she had to balance the creativity of painting with what she considered to be the more frustrating, mundane job of being a dean's wife. Inspired by the high plains and Rocky Mountains, she created highly energized landscapes using intense colors, often in ripple-like patterns. "What really motivated me … was my desire to captivate everything," she wrote. "I put on canvas an eagerness to possess the wonder of nature and beauty of color and line—to encompass everything, not to let anything escape." At the same time, she remained concerned about the disappearing natural landscape as powerful postwar development unfolded.

KEY PAINTERS

Muriel Sibell Wolle (1898–1977). The daughter of a Brooklyn architect, Muriel Sibell arrived in Boulder in 1926 to teach in the new art department of the university. A year later, she became head of the department, a position she held for the next 20 years. Soon after her arrival, she took a bus trip to Central City and Black Hawk. It changed her life.

As she wrote in the preface of her landmark book, *Stampede to Timberline*, "As the result of one ride, I dedicated myself to recording pictorially the mining towns of the state before they disappeared, or before those which are still active were 'restored' past all semblance of their past glory; and almost without knowing it, I was also deep in history."

Some of her friends from the Colorado Mountain Club's Boulder Group drove her on rough jeep roads to her subjects. She developed a shorthand, often doing a quick sketch, which she completed at her leisure (sometimes years later) in lithographic crayon. Occasionally she used color. In 1945, she married Professor of English Francis Wolle. He encouraged her to turn her drawings and historical research into a book. As a result, in 1949, 22 years and 240 mining camps later, she published *Stampede to Timberline*. Since then, many of the buildings and towns she documented have vanished, making her artistic record all the more valuable.

Muriel Sibell Wolle. Here depicted while painting by a fence in the company of her less-than-interested dog, Muriel Sibell Wolle created an immense, highly distinctive group of sketches and paintings that featured Colorado's largely abandoned mining towns crumbing into ruin as the once-great industry died away in the 20th century.

Photograph by Victoria Barker.
Courtesy of Archives, University of Colorado at Boulder Libraries.

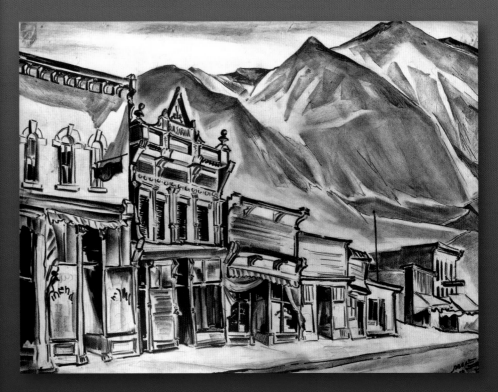

Telluride Scene in 1962. Once one of Colorado's most important mining towns, Telluride was crumbling into ruin when Sibell Wolle captured this street scene. Skiing restored the town's vitality in the later 20th century.

Painting by Muriel Sibell Wolle. Courtesy of Janet and David Robertson.

KEY PAINTERS

William Sanderson (1905–1990). Born in Latvia, William Sanderson lived in the Russian Empire until the age of 18. He and his family immigrated to the United States in 1923. While living in New York, he studied art and became an illustrator for some of the most prominent American magazines of the early 20th century. Sanderson was stationed at Lowry Field in Denver during World War II. After the war, he returned to Denver, and Vance Kirkland hired him to teach advertising design at the University of Denver School of Art. After becoming a professor there, he began his painting career. Sanderson's paintings represent a variety of styles, making him one of the most important figures in postwar Colorado art.

January 1965. A native of Latvia, William Sanderson became one of Colorado's most influential artists, using a spare, modernist style influenced by cubism, surrealism, and regionalism.

Painting by William Sanderson. Private Collection.

KEY PAINTERS

Buffalo Kaplinski (1943–). Born in Chicago, Buffalo Kaplinski attended the Art Institute of Chicago and became a commercial illustrator before abandoning that career and moving to Taos, New Mexico, where he transformed his creative life through the Taos Society of Artists, and settled in Elizabeth, Colorado, on the plains east of Denver. His work reflects a modernist approach to the West and Southwest and many other places, through his use of brilliant colors to depict mountains and desert landscapes, coupled with a pointillistic approach to detail. Working in oils, acrylics, and watercolors, his unique style presents a bold, quasi-abstract interpretation of the immense vistas of the region.

St. Elmo's Autumn. The high slopes of Mount Princeton tower over the changing aspen set in a forest of evergreens near the old mining town of St. Elmo in this characteristic painting by Buffalo Kaplinski. Though Kaplinski was eclectic in his choice of subject matter, a reflection of his global travel, his work formed one of the most distinctive, dramatic, and significant styles in the broad panorama of Colorado art.

Painting by Buffalo Kaplinski. Private Collection.

KEY PAINTERS

Sushe Felix (1958–) and **Tracy Felix (1957–).** The husband and wife team of Tracy Felix and Sushe Felix became major interpreters of western mountain landscapes through modernist styles. Sushe Felix drew inspiration from the Transcendental Painting Group in Santa Fe, and her work used the brilliant colors from acrylics "to create an orderly composition of both geometric and organic form." She achieved movement in her works "by repeating forms, shapes, and different directions of line ... to depict the natural rhythms of life and nature." Tracy Felix, who grew up in southern Colorado and hiked and skied its mountains, observed that his paintings were all about "expressing [his] love for the western landscape. The mountain peaks, wild cloud forms, the expansive sky and incredible geology" comprise the essentials in his paintings, unique for their bold representation, blue-green-brown colorations, and powerful clouds towering over the landscape.

The Storm. Clouds and rain engulf the high peaks in this cubist-like work of Sushe Felix. _Painting by Sushe Felix. Private Collection._

Capitol Peak. Billowing clouds developing into thunderheads towering over a spare blue, green, and brown mountainscape, sometimes with a lake or river, informs Tracy Felix's interpretations of the Rockies.

Painting by Tracy Felix. Private Collection.

Rifle Gap Curtain. The artwork shown here, by Christo and Jeanne-Claude (Christo Vladimiroff Jovacheff and Jeanne-Claude Renat de Guillabon), is the only Colorado artwork to require an environmental impact statement. Christo and Jeanne-Claude's breathtaking orange curtain across Rifle Gap became one of the most controversial works of art in Colorado history. It stood for only about 28 hours before the approach of bad weather forced the artists to remove it.

Photograph by Dwane Howell. Courtesy of Dwane Howell.

American Fable. Burgeoning economic activity along the Front Range of the Rockies pushed housing construction into the mountains, with the consequent development of new subdivisions on innumerable hillsides. All this made growth a controversial public issue in the later 20th century, a controversy reflected in late 20th-century art, such as in this work by Chuck Forsman.

Painting by Chuck Forsman. Courtesy of Gerald Peters Gallery, Santa Fe, New Mexico.

Hidden Snowmass Valley, 2007. The Elk Mountains of western Colorado form the larger setting for this inspired landscape. "Working outdoors assures me of two things," writes Duesberry, "absolute concentration and a sense of urgency which causes me to distill the land to irreducible forms."

Painting by Joellyn Duesberry. Courtesy of Joellyn Duesberry.

GLANCING BACK

JAMES E. FELL, JR.

———

Colorado's mountains and mountaineers had a powerful impact on the Centennial State in the course of the 20th century, but it was one far different from any previous time in its history. Building off the routes blazed by ancient peoples and the myriad achievements of 19th-century pioneers, new generations formalized much of what had gone before. Earlier peoples had kept routes and trails in their heads, eventually depicting them on maps; those of the 20th century made increasingly accurate maps, determined far more accurate heights, and used ever more sophisticated technologies to pinpoint routes, distances, and special features.

Early mountaineers had climbed in less formal, perhaps haphazard ways, whereas their successors in the 20th century created more systematic approaches to mountaineering. Preceding generations had found it difficult to access the mountains by train, horse, or shanks mare, but 20th-century enthusiasts enjoyed the greater accessibility provided by cars and paved roads, newer skis, aircraft, and superhighways. And while 19th-century adventurers had adapted equipment designed for anything but mountaineering, their 20th-century compatriots benefited from clothing and equipment of every sort designed especially for hiking, climbing, and skiing.

With these advances also came the systematic management of the lands and the landscape. The creation of the US Forest Service, the National Park Service, and other state and federal agencies, along with specific programs, brought government regulation and scientific management to the mountains,

Descending from a Soft Sky. A climber descends the South Ridge of Maroon Peak after a stormy traverse of the Maroon Bells.

Paintings by James Disney. Courtesy of James Disney.

although those agencies and efforts also bent to the vicissitudes of political life at local, state, and national levels. And all those influences sometimes produced controversies over differing views of the mountains, the landscapes, and the utilization of their vast natural resources. The mountains did not exist in a vacuum, and the questions of who managed the lands, for what purpose, and in whose interest sometimes led to conflict. But the steady advance of tourism as an industry and environmentalism as mainstream thought in American society served to preserve and protect the high country and its ecosystems.

Throughout the 20th century and into the 21st, the Colorado Mountain Club and its members played key roles in these developments. From its founding in 1912, the club proved instrumental in the founding of Rocky Mountain National Park and the creation of other outdoor preserves for hiking, skiing, and mountaineering in all its forms. Its members led the way in developing and maintaining routes to summits, lakes, and other natural features; lent expertise to develop new equipment; and helped open the mountains to the enjoyment of many others. And the club and its members played important roles in cultural development in the high country as well as in the preservation and protection of the larger environment. President Theodore Roosevelt once proclaimed the value of what he called "the strenuous life" in the outdoors; the Colorado Rockies became a centerpiece of that life for many Americans and people from other lands.

Mount Evans. Named for Colorado's second and most important territorial governor, John Evans, this Fourteener dominates the skyline west of Denver and forms a key element in mountaineering in the metropolitan Denver area.

Reduction woodblock print by Leon Loughridge.

Courtesy of Leon Loughridge.

East Beckwith Mountain Reflected in Lost Lake Slough. Autumn color makes this area around Kebler Pass a favorite among photographers.

Photograph by Dave Cooper. Courtesy of Dave Cooper.

ABOUT THE COLORADO MOUNTAIN CLUB

DAVID HITE

MISSION STATEMENT

The mission statement of the Colorado Mountain Club was written in 1912 and has remained unchanged for 100 years.

———

Unite the energy, interest, and knowledge of the students, explorers, and lovers of the mountains of Colorado;

Collect and disseminate information regarding the Rocky Mountains on behalf of science, literature, art, and recreation;

Stimulate public interest in our mountain area;

Encourage the preservation of forests, flowers, fauna, and natural scenery; and

Render readily accessible the alpine attractions of this region.

———

COLORADO MOUNTAIN CLUB PRESIDENTS

1912–1916	James G. Rogers	1957	Elwyn A. Arps	1983	Glenn Porzak
1917–1918	H. F. Brooks	1958	Paul W. Gorham	1984	Pieter Hondius
1919–1920	George C. Barnard	1959	James C. Gamble	1985	Arthur Porter
1921–1923	George H. Harvey, Jr.	1960	Lester Michel	1986	Albert Ossinger
1924	Edwin H. Perkins	1961	Florian A. Cajori	1987	Richard Jones
1925	Edmund B. Rogers	1962	Kenneth R. Wright	1988	Gary Grange
1926	Carl Blaurock	1963	Fred G. Barton	1989	Susan Baker
1927	Edmund B. Rogers	1964	Jack McDowell	1990	Donald Langmuir
1928–1929	L. R. Kendrick	1965	Allen Greene	1991	Russell Hayes
1930–1931	Lewis E. Perkins	1966	Bruce G. Sommers	1992	John Verbiscar
1932	Carl Blaurock	1967	Allen Auten	1993	Gerald Caplan
1933	L. R. Kendrick	1968	Fred Ruckhaus	1994	Mary Ann Davitt
1934–1935	Garrat B. Van Wagenen	1969	David A. Carter	1995	Dan Bereck
1936	David Rosendale	1970	Clinton M. Kelley	1996	Steven Bragg
1937	H. M. Walters	1971	Sam Alfend	1997	Sterling Drumwright
1938	Carl Blaurock	1972	Carl Brandauer	1998	Gene Gebow
1939	C. Earl Davis	1973	Hugh E. Kingery	1999	Sherry Richardson
1940–1942	Harvey T. Sethman	1974	Bobby Bracewell	2000	Susan Baker
1943–1945	Malcolm Lindsey	1975	John Devitt	2001	Rolf Asphaug
1946	Herb Hollister	1976	Walter Jessel	2002	Bill Houghton
1947–1950	Henry A. Buchtel	1977	Gudrun Gaskill	2003	Steven Bragg
1951	Roy R. Murchison	1978	David Waddington	2004	Sherry Richardson
1952–1953	Howard W. Brewer	1979	Fred Ruckhaus	2005	Lon Carpenter
1954	Vaughn E. Ham	1980	Gale Kehmeier	2006–2008	Janice Heidel
1955	Donald E. Peel	1981	W. A. (Alan) Delamere	2009–2010	Wynne Whyman
1956	Robert W. Ellingwood	1982	George Saum	2011–	Alice White

ALBERT ELLINGWOOD GOLDEN ICE AX MOUNTAINEERING ACHIEVEMENT AWARD

This award is given to Colorado Mountain Club members who have distinguished themselves in mountaineering and inspired club members to follow in their paths.

2002	Jim Gehres	2007	Bob Martin
2003	Terry Root	2008	Jack DePagter
2004	Glenn Porzak	2009	Jean Aschenbrenner
2005	Gary Neptune	2010	Dale Johnson
2006	Gerry Roach		

CARL BLAUROCK SILVER PITON AWARD

This award is given to Colorado Mountain Club members who have invested a substantial amount of effort in CMC activities resulting cumulatively in significant improvement to the Club.

1996	Gerald Caplan	2004	Sherry Richardson
1997	Susan Baker	2005	John Devitt
1998	Dan Bereck	2006	Steve Bonowski
1999	Chip Drumwright	2007	Madeline Framson
2000	Steve Bragg	2008	Giles Toll
2001	Russ Hayes	2009	Jack Reed
2002	Jan Robertson	2010	Walt Borneman
2003	Al Ossinger		

COLORADO MOUNTAIN CLUB
TIMELINE

—◁▯▷—

THE EARLY YEARS—1912–1919

► On April 26, 1912, 25 charter members meet in a ballroom of a Denver Capitol Hill home to establish the Colorado Mountain Club. Two days later the first club trip is made to the Cheesman Park Pavilion followed by a first hike to South Boulder Peak on May 30.

► Annual outings begin in 1912, the first to the upper valley of Bear Creek near Mount Evans, followed by a 1914 outing to Rocky Mountain National Park's Never Summer Range. In 1915 Rocky Mountain National Park is dedicated, with the CMC having played a significant role in its establishment.

► Summer outings continue: in 1916 to Wild Basin and in 1917 to Ashcroft.

► *Trail & Timberline*, the club's official publication, first appears in 1918 with a printing of 437 copies.

► In 1919, the Pikes Peak Group in Colorado Springs becomes a part of the club.

► By decade's end, the membership soars to 450 people. Annual dues are $3.50.

The First Outing, the Last of the Campers atop Mount Evans, August 29, 1912. The week-long itinerary included climbing three mountains, transportation by train and horse-drawn stage to the area, meals, and camp supplies, all for $14.15. Pictured are (from left to right) George Harvey, Elvia Harvey, James Grafton Rogers, Warren Barnard (top), Keith Ferguson (bottom), George Barnard (top), probably Emma Barnard, two unidentified individuals, and likely Lucretia Vaile.

Courtesy of Colorado Mountain Club Archives.

THE TWENTIES

► The decade sees growth in membership, establishment of new groups along the Front Range, more summer outings, and significant first ascents by club members.

► The Boulder Group is founded in 1920, followed by the Fort Collins Group and the Shining Mountain Group in Estes Park in 1922.

► By 1922, the club has 1,100 members, growing to 1,300 by the next year. Annual state dues are $4.

► Locations for outings become statewide. In 1920, 84 members hike into Chicago Basin and other San Juan locations, while others gather at Snowmass Lake and in the Sangre de Cristo Range. In 1926, a club group travels to Glacier National Park. In 1929, a CMC group hikes into the Uncompahgre–Wetterhorn area.

► Two of the CMC's notable early figures, Carl Blaurock and Bill Ervin, finish climbing all the Fourteeners. Other firsts include an ascent of the east face of Longs Peak by seven members along the route christened "Broadway," and Steve Hart, Bill Ervin, and Carl Blaurock's climb of Lone Eagle Peak in 1929, a year during which rope becomes popular for climbing.

► In 1925, the CMC publishes John L. Jerome Hart's *Fourteen Thousand Feet*, the first comprehensive history of Colorado mountaineering, and in 1928 *Encyclopaedia Britannica* recognizes the club as the "mountain authority."

► In 1928, the Boulder Group built the Brainard Cabin, still in use today.

1927 Needles Outing. Twenty-one of the 24 climbers to reach the summit of Mount Eolus during the Colorado Mountain Club's 16th Annual Summer Outing—the Club's second official trip to the Needle Mountains.

Courtesy of Colorado Mountain Club Archives.

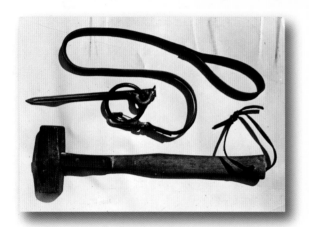

Piton and Piton Hammer before the 1960s. The piton was used as early as 1850 in Europe. By the early 1900s in the United States it was reduced in weight and size and composed of malleable soft iron or steel. A hook (pictured here) or a carabiner provided linkage to a climbing rope. When hammered into rock, a piton would conform to the crack but had limited re-usability. By the 1960s, pitons were made of alloy steel, stronger, easily re-usable, and removable. Modern pitons are composed of either stamp-cut or forged metal alloy, aluminum, hardened chromium-molybdenum steel, or even titanium alloy. Entirely flat surface metal pitons with the eye flush to the blade on the piton are seldom used today.

Courtesy of Colorado Mountain Club Archives.

THE THIRTIES AND FORTIES

► Through difficult economic times resulting in a membership drop to 416 in 1934, the club continues to offer hikes and climbs and conduct winter and summer outings as well as increase the number of its groups and expand its influence. Winter outings are led to Fern Lake in 1932, 1933, and 1934. Summer outings extend to Wyoming's Wind River Range in 1930, Snowmass in 1933 and 1934, and the Gore Range in 1935.

► In 1932 the federal government's Bureau of Land Management announces its intention to keep Berthoud Pass open all winter; in 1933 the Denver Group opens First Creek Cabin.

► In 1935 in southern Colorado, the Huerfano Group forms.

► In 1936 the CMC begins operating a ski bus to Berthoud Pass: $1.75 round-trip.

► The year 1937 sees the first CMC president elected from outside the Denver Group, followed in 1938 by the Denver Group's formal establishment. As the Denver Group's membership continues to grow, it initiates a hiking classification system.

► During 1938, in part through the work of the CMC, Dinosaur National Monument is expanded.

► The Denver Juniors evolve in the 1930s for young mountaineers, 14 to 21 years old, their trips led by adults in the CMC. While the pranks, hi-jinks, and games are sometimes pretty wild—and prompt an annual, zany issue of *Trail & Timberline*—many Juniors become skilled mountaineers, and the program becomes a model for other groups.

THE FIFTIES AND SIXTIES

► The post-World War II growth of Colorado contributes to formation of six CMC groups: Western Slope in 1951; Aspen in 1964; El Pueblo, Longmont, and Longs Peak in 1963; and San Juan in 1965.

► Membership grows from 900 in 1952 to 1,250 in 1960.

► The first edition of Robert Ormes's *Guide to the Colorado Mountains* is published in 1952. The club's first winter trip schedule is published in 1954.

► In 1954, the club eliminates the requirement that a person wanting to join be recommended by a qualified member and have climbed a Fourteener.

► The club has outings to the Canadian Rockies, Alaska, and Mount Rainier, and for the first time extends its trips overseas. The Pikes Peak Group acquires a cabin at St. Peters Dome and the Boulder Group builds the Pfiffner Hut.

► The late 1950s see the use of the first palatable freeze-dried food for backpacking; perhaps as a result, in 1961 the club publishes a cookbook.

► In 1964, promoted by the CMC, the Federal Wilderness Act is adopted.

Animas River Crossing, 1947. The Colorado Mountain Club's annual outing of 1947 ventured into the Needle Mountains. The trip began by riding the Durango & Silverton narrow gauge train to the whistle stop at Needleton, followed by the seemingly precarious river crossing, and hiking up to Noname Creek and into a basin giving access to some of the most difficult-to-climb 13,000-foot peaks in Colorado. Sixty years later, only one part of the trip has changed: Climbers now walk across the Animas River on a stable bridge.

Courtesy of Colorado Mountain Club Archives.

THE SEVENTIES AND EIGHTIES

Don't Lean Forward. This group of hikers posed for the photographer on a Colorado Mountain Club trip in the 1940s. By that time the coats, ties, and long skirts of the early 20th century had given way to more comfortable and efficient gear far better suited for mountaineering.

Courtesy of Colorado Mountain Club Archives.

▶ The popularity of mountain recreation fuels growth in the CMC: Club membership grows from 3,500 in 1970 to 7,400 in 1981. Another CMC local group—Estes Park—is formed in 1976. The Boulder Group's Årestua Hut is built in 1970.

▶ The May 1971 issue of *Trail & Timberline* publishes a questionnaire asking members their opinions on hosting the 1976 Winter Olympics in Colorado.

▶ The CMC Foundation is formed in 1973.

▶ In 1974 the club moves into a clubhouse on West Alameda Avenue in Denver.

▶ In 1978 Gudy Gaskill becomes the club's first woman president. She is also the primary force behind the construction of the Colorado Trail, dedicated in 1988. Also in 1978, Pikes Peak Group member Spencer Swanger becomes the first CMC member to climb all 100 highest Colorado peaks.

▶ Three significant books on mountaineering are published during the period: a 75-year history of the Colorado Mountain Club, written by Hugh Kingery; a climbing guide to the Colorado Fourteeners, co-authored by Walter R. Borneman, and Lyn Lampert; and a history of mountaineering in the state entitled *Roof of the Rockies,* by William Bueler.

▶ The creation of wilderness areas is highlighted in 1978 by establishment of the Indian Peaks Wilderness Area. Conservation becomes a focus of the club with the hiring, in 1981, of Anne Vickery as its first conservation director and the CMC Foundation's establishment of the Kindig Fellowship research grant program in 1982.

▶ Peak bagging catches on in the 1980s. The Longs Peak register maintained by the CMC lists 500 summiteers in a single summer week in 1989.

▶ During 1989, the CMC initiates participation in Peak Challenge, an effort to raise funds for the Griffith Center, by sponsoring trips to summit all 54 Fourteeners in one weekend.

High atop Buffalo Peak. These mountaineers take a break for the camera in the midst of a day's hike above Silverthorne near Dillon Reservoir.

Photograph by David Hite. Courtesy of David Hite.

THE NINETIES AND THE FIRST DECADES OF THE 21ST CENTURY

► In 1992, led by CMC president Jerry Capland and AAC president (and former CMC president) Glenn Porzak, the two organizations purchase the closed Golden High School. After a lengthy campaign, enough money is raised for remodeling what becomes the American Mountaineering Center.

► In 1998 the first CMC education director is hired, and in 1999 the Youth Education Program (YEP) is launched. In the same year the club forms a book publishing function in conformance with the club's mission statement.

► Youth groups that began with the Denver Juniors in the 1930s all come to an end by the early 21st century as Colorado College and the Pueblo, Fort Collins, and Boulder groups gradually eliminate their programs. In 2004, the Denver Juniors becomes the last to fade away. Many mountaineers who got their start in these youth groups hold prominent positions, some in professions related to mountaineering.

► In 2004 the club begins receiving financial support from the legislature-established, taxpayer-supported Scientific and Cultural Facilities District. In the same year membership totals 9,100. The club sponsors 3,400 guided hikes; 55 educational programs; 200 schools, seminars, or training sessions; and 29 adventure travel trips within Colorado and around the world.

Kendell on Rappel. The Colorado Mountain Club developed its Youth Education Program, or YEP as the acronym goes, to introduce young people to the various skills of mountaineering.

Photograph by Brenda Porter. Courtesy of Brenda Porter.

► In 2005 the CMC website is launched and, by 2007, is used for trip sign-ups for hiking, climbing, skiing, and other club activities. In the same year the 21st Century Circle is established for estate gifts to the CMC.

► A Chaffee County peak is named in honor of Mary Cronin, the first woman to climb all the Fourteeners.

► The year 2008 sees the opening of the Bradford Washburn American Mountaineering Museum, the only comprehensive mountaineering museum in North America.

► In 2009 *Trail & Timberline* publishes issue number 1001.

► A 2009 CMC conservation effort leads support for passage of state regulations for off-highway vehicles on federal land, and Rocky Mountain National Park's backcountry is designated as wilderness. In addition, the Dominguez Escalante National Conservation Area is established.

► The year 2010 witnesses the establishment of the American Mountaineering Museum Hall of Mountaineering Excellence Awards. The first honorees are Yvon Chouinard, Robert Craig, Robert Bates, and Dr. Charles Houston.

► By decade's end, the club hires its first full-time marketing director.

► In 2012, the Colorado Mountain Club celebrates its 100th anniversary as the leading hiking and mountaineering club in Colorado.

Waxing Skis. Cross-country skiing required correct waxing to adjust to winter temperatures until the development of fish-scale skis in the later 20th century.

Photograph by Janet N. Robertson. Courtesy of Janet N. Robertson.

Bradford Washburn American Mountaineering Museum. Step over the crevasse as you enter the world of the mountaineer. You'll experience the technical challenges of the high mountains, hear the climbers tell their stories, see the tools of climbing yesterday and today, and much more.

Photograph by Dan Hamm. Exhibit design by Quatrefoil Associates.

THE AMERICAN MOUNTAINEERING CENTER

Mount Everest Model. The model of Mount Everest shows approaches, climbing routes, and camps on the world's tallest peak. It is used by school groups studying mountaineering history as well as by mountaineers planning expeditions.

Photograph by Christopher J. Case.
Courtesy of Christopher J. Case.

In 1993, the Colorado Mountain Club and the American Alpine Club of New York joined in purchasing and renovating the shuttered Golden High School at 710 10th Street in Golden, Colorado. The result was the creation of the American Mountaineering Center. It houses a 350-seat auditorium; a library devoted to mountaineering; and offices for the Colorado Mountain Club, the American Alpine Club, Outward Bound, and other organizations devoted to the high country. The centerpiece of the building is the Bradford Washburn American Mountaineering Museum, created by the Colorado Mountain Club, the American Alpine Club, and the National Geographic Society. It is the only museum in the United States that offers a comprehensive interpretation of mountaineering past and present.

Hagerman Peak. Clouds float over the imposing summit of Hagerman Peak in the Maroon Bells–Snowmass Wilderness Area in the Elk Mountains near Aspen. This was one of the first five wilderness areas in Colorado created by the Wilderness Act of 1964.

Photograph by Dave Cooper. Courtesy of Dave Cooper.

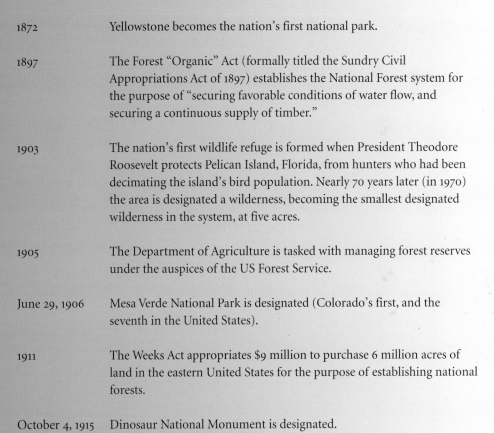

AN ENVIRONMENTAL TIMELINE

1872	Yellowstone becomes the nation's first national park.
1897	The Forest "Organic" Act (formally titled the Sundry Civil Appropriations Act of 1897) establishes the National Forest system for the purpose of "securing favorable conditions of water flow, and securing a continuous supply of timber."
1903	The nation's first wildlife refuge is formed when President Theodore Roosevelt protects Pelican Island, Florida, from hunters who had been decimating the island's bird population. Nearly 70 years later (in 1970) the area is designated a wilderness, becoming the smallest designated wilderness in the system, at five acres.
1905	The Department of Agriculture is tasked with managing forest reserves under the auspices of the US Forest Service.
June 29, 1906	Mesa Verde National Park is designated (Colorado's first, and the seventh in the United States).
1911	The Weeks Act appropriates $9 million to purchase 6 million acres of land in the eastern United States for the purpose of establishing national forests.
October 4, 1915	Dinosaur National Monument is designated.

August 25, 1916	The National Park Organic Act creates the National Park Service and establishes the National Park System in order to conserve scenery, wildlife, and "historic objects" for future generations.
1924	Ecologist Aldo Leopold achieves designation of the first official wilderness area—the Gila Wilderness in New Mexico.
1934	The CMC reconnaissance flight over Dinosaur National Monument takes place.
1936	The CMC organizes Canyon of Lodore–Yampa River Reconnaissance trips.
1938	Dinosaur National Monument is expanded to 204,000 acres.
1946	The Grazing Service and the General Land Office are merged to form the Bureau of Land Management.
1956	The Colorado River Water Project Act is enacted.
1960	The Multiple Use and Sustained Yield Act redefines the purpose of the national forests to include not only timber and watershed concerns but also recreation, wildlife, fishing, hunting, and soil concerns.
1962	Roger Fuehrer attends the Sierra Club convention.
September 3, 1964	The Wilderness Act is signed into law on September 3, designating 9.1 million acres as wilderness throughout the United States, including La Garita, Maroon Bells–Snowmass, Mount Zirkel, Rawah, and West Elk wilderness areas in Colorado.
1964	The Land and Water Conservation Fund Act is established to purchase park and refuge lands with royalties from offshore oil drilling.
August 1966	The CMC calls for protection of Florissant Fossil Beds against housing development.
October 2, 1968	The National Wild and Scenic Rivers Act is enacted.
August 20, 1969	The Florissant Fossil Beds National Monument is designated.
January 1, 1970	The National Environmental Policy Act is signed into law, requiring an analysis of the environmental impacts of federal actions.
1970	The Environmental Protection Agency is established. The Clean Air Act is signed into law. The President's Council on Environmental Quality is established. It advises and assists the president on environmental policies and oversees the implementation of the environmental impact assessment process by federal agencies.

1972	The Clean Water Act is signed into law.
1973	The Endangered Species Act is signed into law, protecting habitat for plants and wildlife.
1974	The Forest and Rangeland Renewable Resources Planning Act establishes a planning process for all forest and rangeland resources.
1975	Flat Tops and Weminuche wilderness areas are designated.
1976	The National Forest Management Act requires the US Forest Service to include economic, wildlife, wilderness, and recreational uses in planning.
	The Black Canyon of the Gunnison, Great Sand Dunes, Eagles Nest, and Mesa Verde wilderness areas are designated, and more than 1.7 million acres of wilderness are designated in 19 other states.
	The Federal Lands Policy and Management Act governs the use of the national lands managed by the Bureau of Land Management.
1978	Hunter-Fryingpan and Indian Peaks wilderness areas are designated, and more than 5.5 million acres of wilderness are designated in 17 other states.

1980	The Neota, Never Summer, Raggeds, Lizard Head, Lost Creek, Mount Evans, Mount Massive, Mount Sneffels, Cache La Poudre, Collegiate Peaks, Comanche Peak, Holy Cross, South San Juan, and Uncompahgre wilderness areas are designated. A number of other existing areas gain considerable additions.
1981	The CMC hires Anne Vickery as its first paid conservation staff member.
1984	New wilderness areas totaling 8.6 million acres are established in 21 states. Colorado gains a small portion of the Platte River Wilderness, the majority of which is established in Wyoming.
1993	The Colorado Wilderness Act of 1993 establishes Buffalo Peaks, Byers Peak, Fossil Ridge, Greenhorn Mountain, Powderhorn, Ptarmigan Peak, Sangre de Cristo, Sarvis Creek, and Vasquez Peak wilderness areas.
1998	President Bill Clinton issues his directive to the US Forest Service to conduct an Environmental Impact Statement leading to possible long-term protection of 50 million to 60 million acres of roadless lands.
1999	The Black Canyon of the Gunnison National Monument is designated a national park.

The Gates Hut. Bicyclists approach the Gates Hut toward the end of a strenuous day pedaling through the mountains.

Photograph by David Hiser. Courtesy of David Hiser.

2000	The Black Ridge Canyons Wilderness Area is designated; the bill also creates the adjacent Colorado Canyons National Conservation Area.
	The Black Canyon of the Gunnison Wilderness Area is expanded.
	The Gunnison Gorge Wilderness Area is designated.
	The Spanish Peaks Wilderness Area is designated. The area had been studied and considered for wilderness designation for nearly two decades.
2001	The James Peak Wilderness Area is designated.
2004	Initially set aside as a national monument in 1932, Great Sand Dunes National Park is designated, embracing some 107,000 acres and reaching from the flats of the San Luis Valley to the 14,165-foot summit of Kit Carson Mountain.
March 30, 2009	The backcountry of Rocky Mountain National Park and Dominguez Canyon wilderness areas designated.

ENDNOTES

PROLOGUE

1. Zebulon M. Pike, *An Account of Expeditions to the Sources of the Mississippi and through the Western Parts of Louisiana* (Philadelphia, PA: C. & A. Conrad, 1810); Donald Jackson, ed., *The Journals of Zebulon Montgomery Pike* (Norman: University of Oklahoma Press, 1966).

2. Edwin James, *Account of an Expedition from Pittsburgh to the Rocky Mountains . . . 1819 and 1920 . . . under the Command of Major Stephen H. Long*, edited by Reuben Gold Thwaites (New York: Arno Press, 1966).

3. Janet Robertson, *The Magnificent Mountain Women: Adventures in the Colorado Rockies* (Lincoln: University of Nebraska Press, 2003), pp. 2–6; Agnes Wright Spring, *A Bloomer Girl on Pikes Peak 1858* (Denver, CO: Denver Public Library, 1949).

4. Isabella Bird, *A Lady's Life in the Rocky Mountains* (Norman: University of Oklahoma Press, 1960), pp. 92–101.

CHAPTER 1

1. Patricia M. Fazio, "Cragged Crusade: The Fight for Rocky Mountain National Park, 1909–1915" (MS thesis, University of Wyoming, 1982), pp. 111, 112; Lucretia Vaile, "Auditing the Club Scrapbooks with Personal Observations and Reminiscences from Many Sources," *Trail & Timberline* (1922), pp. 1–6.

2. Elinor Bluemel, *Florence Sabin: Colorado Woman of the Century* (Boulder: University of Colorado Press, 1959), p. 144.

3. James Grafton Rogers, "The Creation of Rocky Mountain Park," *Trail & Timberline* (June 1965), p. 99; Fazio, p. 5; p. 61, quoting letter from Rogers to "Mr. Stone," light-green scrapbook, Enos Mills Cabin Collection, Estes Park, Colorado.

4. Rogers, p. 100; Louisa Ward Arps and Elinor Eppich Kingery, assisted by Hugh E. Kingery, *High Country Names* (Estes Park, CO: The Rocky Mountain Nature Association, 1977), p. 1; Rogers, p. 100.

5. Harriet Vaille Bouck, "Arapaho Hunting Grounds Revisited," *Trail & Timberline* (June 1965), pp. 105–7; Arps and Kingery, pp. 123, 136–37, 195; Rogers, p. 101.

6. Fazio, pp. 150–85.

7. Alexander Drummond, *Enos Mills: Citizen of Nature* (Boulder: University Press of Colorado, 1995), p. 22; Carl Abbott, "The Active Force: Enos A. Mills and the National Park Movement," *The Colorado Magazine* (Winter/Spring 1978), p. 80; Rogers, p. 99; Granville Liles, gleaned from a talk he gave to the CMC's state board on May 14, 1965, *Trail & Timberline* (June 1965), p. 123; Rogers, p. 101.

CHAPTER 2

1. William M. Bueler, *Roof of the Rockies: A History of Colorado Mountaineering*, 3rd ed. (Golden: Colorado Mountain Club Press, 2000), pp. 64, 77, 156, 159–63, 169.

2. Albert R. Ellingwood, "Climbing in the Sangre de Cristo," *Trail & Timberline* (June 1925), pp. 1–5.

3. Ellingwood, "The Eastern Arête of the Crestone Needle," *Trail & Timberline* (November 1925), pp. 6–9; Ellingwood's obituary is in *Trail & Timberline* (June 1934), pp. 81, 85.

4. Bueler, pp. 217–18; *Denver Post*, July 7, 1976, and September 1, 1976; "They won't let" in *Rocky Mountain News*, June 29, 1939.

5. Bueler, pp. 152–55; Albert R. Ellingwood, *Outing Magazine* (November 1921); Bueler, pp. 88–89; Carl Blaurock, "Climb of Mount Lindbergh," *Trail & Timberline* (November 1929), pp. 10–11.

6. Woody Smith, "Climbing the 'High Tops' with Mary Cronin and the Colorado Mountain Club," *Colorado Heritage* (Autumn 2008), pp. 50–63.

CHAPTER 3

1. *Trail & Timberline* (August 1942), p. 103; Dale L. Johnson, "Two New Routes on the Maiden," *Trail & Timberline* (August 1955), pp. 139–142.

2. Mark Scott-Nash, *Playing for Real: Stories from Rocky Mountain Rescue* (Golden, CO: CMC Press, 2007); Hugh Kingery, *The Colorado Mountain Club* (Evergreen, CO: Cordillera Press, 1988), p. 59.

3. David Rearick, "The First Ascent of the Diamond, East Face of Longs Peak," *American Alpine Journal,* Vol. 12 (1961), pp. 297–301; "Stunt and Daring" in Steve Roper and Allen Steck, *Fifty Classic Climbs of North America* (London: Diadem, 1979), p. 203.

4. Jack Fralick, "East Face of Monitor Peak," *Trail & Timberline* (December 1947), pp. 191–195; Bill E. Forrest, "Colorado," *American Alpine Journal,* Issue 47 (1973), pp. 430–432.

5. "Could I Really" in Layton Kor, "Early Days," *Climbing,* No. 79 (August 1983), p. 12; Steve Komito, "Layton Kor," *Climbing,* No. 113 (April 1989), p. 70; Ed Webster, "The Book of Kor," *Climbing,* (June 1988), pp. 50–58.

CHAPTER 4

1. *Trail & Timberline,* No. 205 (November 1935).

2. *Trail & Timberline,* No. 219 (January 1937).

3. Janet N. Robertson, personal correspondence with the author, July 2009.

4. *Trail & Timberline,* No. 480 (December 1958); *Trail & Timberline,* No. 517 (January 1962); *Trail & Timberline,* No. 759 (April 1982); *Trail & Timberline,* No. 572 (August 1966); *Trail & Timberline,* No. 621 (September 1970); *Trail & Timberline,* No. 715 (August 1978); *Trail & Timberline,* No. 736 (May 1980).

5. Frederick Chapin, *Mountaineering in Colorado* (Boston: Appalachian Mountain Club, 1889), pp. 97, 98; Louisa Ward Arps and Elinor Eppich Kingery, assisted by Hugh E. Kingery, *High Country Names* (Denver: Colorado Mountain Club, 1966), pp. 166, 167.

6. R. Scott Rappold, "Dust in Snow Causes Early Melting in Region's High Country," *The Gazette* (Colorado Springs, CO), April 17, 2010; Thomas H. Painter, Jeffrey S. Deems, Jayne Belnap, Alan F. Harnet, Christopher C. Landry, and Bradley Udall, "Response of Colorado River Runoff to Dust Radiative Forcing in Snow," *Proceedings of the National Academy of Sciences* (September 2010), doi: 10.1073/pnas.0913139107.

CHAPTER 5

1. Jack A. Benson, "Before Aspen and Vail: The Story of Recreational Skiing in Frontier Colorado," *Journal of the West,* 22 (January 1983), pp. 52–63.

2. Jack A. Benson, "Before Skiing Was Fun," *Western Historical Quarterly,* 15 (April 1984), pp. 163 –74; Stanley Dempsey and James E. Fell, Jr., *Mining the Summit: Colorado's Ten Mile District, 1860–1960* (Norman: University of Oklahoma Press, 1986), pp. 47–49; Annie Gilbert Coleman, *Ski Style: Sport and Culture in the Rockies* (Lawrence: University Press of Kansas, 2004), pp. 21–22.

3. Benson, "Before Skiing Was Fun," pp. 163–74; Coleman, pp. 13–40.

4. Janet Robertson, *The Magnificent Mountain Women: Adventures in the Colorado Rockies* (Lincoln: University of Nebraska Press, 2003), pp. 36–44.

5. Coleman, pp. 41–72, 134.

6. Abbott Fay, *Ski Tracks in the Rockies: A Century of Colorado Skiing* (Evergreen CO: Cordillera Press, 1984).

Harbinger. When the ptarmigan begin to change their mottled brown plumage to all white plumage, they are the harbinger of winter in Colorado's high country.

Painting by James Disney. Courtesy of James Disney.

ABOUT THE AUTHORS

JANET NEUHOFF ROBERTSON's family started visiting what is now Rocky Mountain National Park in 1910. A native of St. Louis, Missouri, she began spending her summers in the Estes Park area at the age of two. In 1952, she and her father joined the Colorado Mountain Club, mostly so they could climb Fourteeners. A few years later, she met David Robertson, who was her CMC rock-climbing instructor. They married in 1956 and raised their three children to love the outdoors as they did. Robertson is a writer/photographer whose best-known book is *Magnificent Mountain Women: Adventures in the Colorado Rockies.*

JAMES E. FELL, JR., jetted to Colorado in 1967 to attend summer school in Boulder and within an hour or so of arrival knew that he had come "home to a place he'd never been before," to quote the songwriter John Denver. A native of Fall River, Massachusetts, Fell grew up in New England, but has spent most of his life in the Centennial State teaching history at various colleges and universities and sometimes working in the private sector. He is a leader in the Denver Group of the Colorado Mountain Club, a former director of the organization, a member of various committees, and author or co-author of several books and articles.

DAVID HITE is a Colorado native and a 25-year member of the Colorado Mountain Club. He has served in many volunteer positions for the organization and is on the board of directors of the Colorado Mountain Club Foundation. As a photographer, his work has appeared in CMC publications and exhibits. For this publication he researched, identified, gathered, and cataloged the book's images.

CHRISTOPHER J. CASE served as the first creative director for the Bradford Washburn American Mountaineering Museum from 2006 to 2008. He then became editor and director of photography and design for *Trail & Timberline*, the magazine of the Colorado Mountain Club. As a photographer and writer, he has worked for newspapers, national magazines, and national conservation organizations.

WALTER R. BORNEMAN is best known in Colorado's mountaineering community as the co-author of *A Climbing Guide to Colorado's Fourteeners*, first published in 1978 and in print for 25 years. Borneman served as the first chairman of the Colorado Fourteeners Initiative and on the board of the Colorado Mountain Club Foundation. He is the author of 10 books and numerous articles about mountains, railroads, and the American West, most recently publishing *Rival Rails: The Race to Build America's Greatest Transcontinental Railroad*.

INDEX

The Summit. Climbers have erected cairns on many summits, such as this one on Andrews Peak in Rocky Mountain National Park.

Painting by James Disney. Courtesy of James Disney.